Oh, For a French Wife!

Oh, for a French Wife!

Cooking by
Ted Moloney and Deke Coleman

Drawings by
George Molnar

ABELARD PRESS / NEW YORK

Acknowledgements

MOLNAR

First of all we kiss the hands of our four French wives whose luncheons and dinners commence on page 101. Whilst Deke and I sat back and suggested, criticized and even rejected, these ladies strove to provide us with the utmost perfection. All of the time they had to compare notes so as not to duplicate each other's recipes. From time to time they tremblingly placed before us superlative luncheons or dinners for our approval. The two luncheons and two dinners we finally approved, and which appear in these pages, are the result.

So to Yanni, Paulette—and may we call you Fabienne?—our deepest thanks. To Louise, our fourth French wife, even extra thanks, for all of her help, both in the kitchen and at the desk, in the selection and final checking of our other recipes. If you know Louise you will know that she is a perfectionist. To our other friends from whom we borrowed, demanded or filched kitchen secrets—Signora Cattani, Madame Horowitz, Eleanor Arrighi, Patricia Volterra, Thelma Tracy, "my sister Evie" and Mike Duval—our thanks again.

Deke commences his part of this book by saying that it would never have been written if he hadn't happened to be drinking a Martini two or three years ago. With this his co-author disagrees. It was really Leon Gellert who commenced this book by giving us our title one Saturday morning four years ago. Mr. Gellert was receiving the first cookbook which Deke and I produced. It was called "The Garrulous Gourmet" (still very much on sale, gracious reader), with recipes provided by a friend in Paris. The title of Mr. Gellert's review was "Oh, for a French Wife!" Could there be a more interesting title for a cookbook? It started us off again. Thank you, Mr. Gellert.

Ted Moloney.

CONTENTS

On the Chemistry
and Philosophy of Cooking

This Section by Lloyd Ring Coleman

HOW CAN YOU COOK WITH AIR? 13
Involving omelettes, Martinis and even the boiling of water
for tea.

WHEREIN I AVOID A CURIOUS MEAL 26
. . . and discuss what heat, fat, salt and a beautiful girl can do
to a filet steak.

PHILOSOPHY OF FRYING 35
Heat peaks of butter, oil, water and dripping and their effects
on food.

OBSERVATIONS ON THE SENSE OF TASTE . . . 66
—and why our palates improve with age.

INTERLUDE 79
Variations on theme of Brillat-Savarin.

YOU CAN'T COOK IN MORE THAN THREE WAYS . . 89
How to get the most out of hot air and oil, and the necessity
for shunning water.

CONTENTS

Soups, Vegetables, Cocktail Parties, Fork Meals, Luncheons and Dinners

COMPLETE WITH RECIPES

This Section by Ted Molonep

COCKTAILS TO COCKCROW 17
    Onion Tart   Quiche Lorraine

A RUSSIAN SOUP 22

SOUP IN THE SUN 30
    French Onion Soup   Creme Vichyssoise

JUST GIVE ME PLAIN HOME COOKING 37
    Beef Casserole

THREE CINDERELLAS 41
    New Potatoes with butter   Souffled Potatoes
    Pommes-de-terre a la Maitre d'Hotel   Onions to serve with Corned Beef
    Duchesse Potatoes   French Fried Onions
    Potatoes Anna   Steamed Cabbage

CONTENTS

FIVE COURSES FOR CONFUCIUS 51
Fried Rice   Sweet and sour Pork
How to Boil Rice Without Making   Sweet and sour Fish
    Glue   Spring Rolls
Chicken and Almonds

JUICE FROM THE CHICKEN 69
Chicken Consomme   Puff Pastry Turnovers

ON THE ROASTING OF CHICKEN 73

TAKING LIBERTIES WITH MARYLAND 75
Fried Chicken into casserole   Sweet Corn Fritters

BEANS AT A BARBECUE 82
Casseroled beans

A CHANGE FROM CURRY 86
Beef Stroganoff   Hungarian Goulash

HOME AT 5:30 93
Globe Artichokes   French Salad
Steak Diane   Cuban Bananas

TWELVE MINUTES FOR SPAGHETTI 98

PERFECT BALANCE IN THE SERVING OF A MEAL . 103

Luncheon by Madame Jean Strauss 107
Creamed Spinach and Eggs   Chicory and Beetroot Salad
Coquilles St. Jacques   Creme Bavaroise
Veal Foyot

Luncheon by Mrs. L. R. Coleman 111
Salad Nicoise   Filet of Beef with Bearnaise Sauce
Chicken Quenelles   Fruit Salad

CONTENTS

Dinner by the Countess D'Espinay 116

Fish Soup   French Salad
Ham Souffle   Riz a l'Imperatrice
Chicken a la Creme

Dinner by Madame Paul Pellier 121

Potage Sante   de-terre Duchesse
Vol-au-vent Financiere   Salad
Saddle of Lamb with Pommes-   Crepes Suzette

Oh, For a French Wife!

"How Can You Cook with Air?"

INVOLVING OMELETTES, MARTINIS AND EVEN
THE BOILING OF WATER FOR TEA

This book wouldn't have happened if I hadn't been drinking
a Martini two or three years ago.

They had a new bartender at the American Club. He

really put his back into it when he shook drinks. Wishing to be helpful to both of us, I said to him,

"You don't shake Martinis."

Evidently that touched him on the raw, for he immediately turned hostile. He said,

"Are you trying to teach me my business?"

"As a matter of fact," I finally came out with, "I am. And that's not all. I can tell you many other things you don't know and should."

"What?" he said, unconsciously trying to draw a red herring across the trail.

"That will come later," I said. "As for the Martini, when you shake it to cool it, you fill it with air. You might as well make it with soda. That would put plenty of air in, and you wouldn't need to work so hard. I do concede," and here I leaned over and whispered to him, "that soda has CO_2 in it, while air is a mixture of O and N and a few rare gases. But they are all gases of one sort or another—and equally bad in a Martini."

"How do you know all that?" he asked, eyeing me suspiciously.

"Easily," I said. "I read the science articles in the Sunday papers." I waved down a protest from him and continued.

"How about those other things? Did you ever realize that the most important ingredient in cooking is air? Yet no cookbook lists air in its index."

"How can you cook with air?" he said, and added, "Do you mean hot air?"

"No," I replied a bit testily. "Have you ever noticed," I continued, "that there is a difference between an omelette that is stirred with the tip of the fork, and one that is beaten? If you love air in an omelette, as you apparently do in a Martini, you do the latter, but if you do, the result will not be the slobbery omelette of France. You can—but it's not advisable—put in baking soda for even more air. I suppose you would like a big puffy one—two thirds air?"

"I hadn't thought of it that way," responded the bartender, thawing out a bit.

"The amount of air makes or unmakes a Martini," I went on. "It makes or unmakes an omelette."

"You must have studied these matters, sir," he said.

"Yes," I agreed. "Food pages in the magazines, weekly broadcasts on food, the Readers' Digest. You can learn from all of them. Take a Hollandaise Sauce. Would you know what that is?"

"Yes sir," he said.

"You surprise me. Well, it curdles. It often does. What do you do? You add a little cold water, remove from the fire and whip it. If you whip it too much it tastes like aerated milk at a milk bar. But you get rid of the curdle."

He looked impressed, so I went on.

"When a cookbook tells you not to roll out dough with one coup de force, it means that the writer is afraid you will roll the air out of it. Cold air going into an oven will chase warm air out of a soufflé and make it sink. When the book says to boil some things with the lid off, it means that air is a necessary ingredient. And if it says to boil things with the lid on, it means that it is a noxious ingredient that takes away those other essential ingredients—vitamins.

"If you boil water for a long time before you make tea, you drive the air out of it and make bad tea.

"Leave freshly ground coffee in the air and what happens? The O_2 in the air carries off the oils that give the tastes. You smell the coffee, but soon you won't be able to taste it. Take the CO_2 out of champagne and beer and what do you have left?"

A newcomer to the bar leaned over to the bartender and whispered, "The answer to that is Sydney beer."

"Presumably the interrupter comes from Melbourne," said I. Then I added another word. "Do you mean to tell me that in all your years of mixing drinks you hadn't even noticed that a shaken Martini was filled with—for a Martini —that useless ingredient—air?"

"No sir, I hadn't," replied the bartender.

"Well, that's where I came in," I said. Still having one learned observation in my locker, I let go with it.

"Those dried lemon peels you use. Their use in flavoring comes from the volatile oils in them that evaporate in a few minutes. It's the air that does it. I'll tell you about oil if you're still here the next time I come back."

With that I slid down off my stool and went out into the night.

Cocktails to Cockcrow

...IN WHICH WE LIFT OUR GLASSES
TO A PAIR OF FAMOUS FRENCH TARTS

Nothing makes a room look emptier than the first arrivals for a cocktail party. Even the Martinis don't do much to bridge the gap until the Lamotte hats and Pellier and Rocher dresses enter, about an hour later than the time for which their owners were invited.

You can try the experiment of asking just a few people in for a drink before dinner, but they still won't believe you and they'll stay on until you feed them.

The last time I tried something of the sort, only eight good friends were invited. I had been precise about the time. "Come before six if you can make it. It's not a party," then trailing off self-consciously on the last few words... "Just a drink on the way home to dinner."

Only George Molnar arrived at six. At seven o'clock a shared hired car brought five more, and they had all been home to change. At seven thirty the final two ladies arrived with cries of "Food! Food!" as I opened the door.

That was my last reactionary stand.

Whether it's eight or forty-eight we're inviting, we might as well be reconciled to the trend of the times.

They'll stay on even though they see that we're getting vengeance by passing around prunes stuffed with cream cheese and those other "savory" bits and pieces that can raise merry hell with stomachs even without cocktails to add to the misery of the morning after.

If we're giving a cocktail party—and who can help it?— let's make the best of the occasion and give them food.

First of all, we'll skip the elaborate savories which take hours to make and often go soggy by the time they're served.

It's so much better to buy long French rolls which cut into slices that can be held easily between the thumb and first finger. We spread plenty of butter on each slice and then, right at the very last minute, we put on them smoked eel with a squeeze of lemon, smoked ham, cold pieces of chicken or lobster with mayonnaise, salami or anything else that has its own good flavor without need of fiddling garnish.

These will be eaten with enthusiasm, and without difficulty, even though they've been so little trouble to prepare.

Also, they've given us the time to work on two masterpieces that are going to be brought in as the climax to our party and not served until they have been seen by all.

These masterpieces are those two wonderful open-faced French tarts known as Quiche Lorraine and Onion Tart.

They are eaten while still warm. Each tart serves ten people.

Either your own flaky pie pastry or ready-made puff pastry rolled thin can be used.

ONION TART

Thinly slice two pounds of white onions and simmer very, very gently in a quarter pound of butter. Keep an eye on them, because not even the edge of a slice must burn. When every piece of onion is soft and floppy, remove from flame and allow to cool.

You might have to add another dab or two of butter as the onions are frying, but don't be in too much of a hurry to do this as onions often give out their liquid rather suddenly, turning an almost dry pan into one well filled with fluid.

1. Mix ½ cup sour cream with 3 well-whisked eggs. Add salt and pepper to taste.
2. Stir all this into the cooled-off onions.
3. Line a 9-inch pie tin with your pastry dough, which should be no more than ⅛ inch thick.
4. Fill this with your onion mixture. Criss-cross the onions with long, thin strips of bacon from which most of the fat has been removed.
5. Bake in a hot oven (425° F.) for 10 minutes; reduce heat to 350° F. for 20 minutes or until the pie crust is nicely golden. When cut into slices, the onion filling holds firm. Serve while still warm.

QUICHE LORRAINE

To give you a picture in advance, this is really an open-faced tart filled with alternate layers of grilled bacon and mild cheese over which you pour an unsweetened custard before placing in the oven.

Half a pound of bacon is sufficient for a round pie tin nine inches in diameter. Lightly grill the bacon, which should be lean.

Line your well-greased pie tin with pastry dough one-eighth inch thick. Start off the filling with a layer of Gruyere cheese. Then a layer of bacon. Cheese again. Bacon again. And so on until you finish with cheese on top.

Over this pour a very rich custard made as follows. Beat together four eggs, a tablespoon of flour, a pinch of salt and a good pinch of nutmeg. Stir in half a pint of cream and one and a half tablespoons of melted butter. Pour over the bacon and cheese until the custard almost reaches the rim of the tart. Bake in a hot oven, 400° F., for ten minutes, then reduce heat to 350° F. and bake about twenty minutes longer or until custard is set.

A Russian Soup

... WHICH GIVES US A NEW RESPECT FOR BEETROOT

When a very attractive girl says, "Ted, I'm going to take you to lunch at the Ritz," well, you go quietly.

This admission doesn't stamp Ted as a gigolo. The lady in question is one of the key women executives in our New York office, a top flight writer and a gourmet.

It was Helen Ridley's knowledge of food that took us to the Ritz, not only for lunch, but to meet the world's most famous chef, Louis Diat.

Only an hour before, I had been standing beside Garbo in one of those plush Fifty-seventh Street picture galleries with a thousand-dollar minimum on oils. This might explain why I cannot remember very much about what must have been an excellent luncheon, except that we had Bortsch.

It was hard to believe that this rich, mildly-red soup was flavored by beetroot. It was as far away in flavor from the vinegary beets that had helped to make Sunday night suppers gloomy for me all through my boyhood, as St. Petersburg is from Sydney.

After the coffee Helen said, "Now for Louis."

More impressed than ever, I followed her down into the sprawling kitchens where Bemelmans used to write amongst the pots and pans when his boss wasn't looking.

Louis Diat, in black coat and striped trousers, greeted us with a smile and a warm handshake that assured me I was not a nuisance.

After a liqueur the tour commenced. What The Old Curiosity Shop is to the readers of Dickens this great basement was to me, who had enjoyed so many chuckles reading "Hotel Splendide." When I mentioned Bemelmans there was a shrug. He was no longer at the Ritz and that was that.

Half an hour later we were back to where we started from. We had talked about kitchens and catering and the wonders of the Ritz, but not one word about l'haute cuisine from the man who, most probably, knows more about it than anyone else in the world today.

Then Louis Diat asked me about toheroa soup which he had never tasted. I had sent some tins of toheroa meat to a friend in New York as a present. I decided to retrieve several and promised them to Louis. One soup led to another. I praised the Bortsch and regretted that eleven thousand miles were about to separate me from it. Didn't I know that Diat had just published his book "Cooking à la Ritz"? The recipe was in it and I should have it.

A phone call was put through to the bookstand in the ground floor vestibule. Down came a page boy with the copy which is beside me as I write. It is inscribed:

"TO MY AUSTRALIAN FRIEND
TED MOLONEY
BEST WISHES FROM LOUIS DIAT. JANUARY 1946."

It was close to four o'clock when we said goodbye and this time, as we shook hands, Louis Diat was very definite that whenever I dined at the Ritz I was to tell the head waiter to send a message to Diat himself that the food was for me.

After that there was one head waiter in New York who greeted me as though I might have been someone of importance.

Flying out to the West Coast I read the Diat recipe for Bortsch and realized why to me it had seemed ambrosia.

It was Bortsch for the Czars. Both duck and beef go into the stock and the balance of the recipe is on an equally magnificent scale.

About twelve months after I returned to Australia I found Bortsch once again. This time the Bortsch was made by Madame Horowitz, a Polish lady who has lived most of her life in Paris. Her Bortsch is a most delectable soup and as it is a recipe for family cooking we are happy to be able to give it to you.

BORTSCH SOUP

2 big onions	2 big carrots
Butter	1 leek
4 lbs. shin of beef	1 turnip
or	1 medium head cabbage
2 lbs. shin and 2 lbs.	4 tomatoes
other boiling beef	3 raw beetroots
Salt, pepper	Sweet or sour cream

Bay leaf, thyme, bouquet garni

Slice onions and brown them in a big pot. Add meat and, when brown, cover with water. Add salt, pepper, bay leaf, a bouquet garni of herbs and thyme. Cook for 1½ to 2 hours.

In another big pot slice very finely carrots, leek, turnip and cabbage. Fry them slowly in butter. When the vegetables are soft and the meat in the other pot nearly tender, take the meat from the pot and strain your stock, clearing it of the onions. Add meat and stock to the vegetables and cook for another 2 hours on a slow fire. Add peeled and sliced tomatoes at the end of the first hour, so that the mixture can cook for another hour together.

A few minutes before the soup is ready, add the beetroots that you have grated. The beetroots must not cook too long, otherwise they will lose their color.

Add sweet or sour cream to the soup before serving.

This is Ukrainian Bortsch. There are different kinds in different parts of Russia. Usually the Bortsch is served with "kulibiak," which is a pastry with minced meat inside like a meat roll. However, the Ritz served pumpernickel which we can buy anywhere, and which is a satisfactory substitute for the mince-meat rolls.

Wherein I Avoid a Curious Meal

MOLNAR

... AND DISCUSS WHAT HEAT, FAT, SALT AND
A BEAUTIFUL GIRL CAN DO TO A FILET STEAK

Business leads me away from home a great deal. This makes me the subject of many varieties in the way of home entertainment—including cooking.

That particular night I was invited to dinner by a physically interesting lass whose husband, like the minstrel boy, to the wars had gone. Not unusually there are advantages in home cooking under these circumstances.

Logically enough we got into the kitchen early. Betty wanted a one-course meal to save time in washing up.

She looked delightful as she got out the black market steak, drippings and the frying pan and put them all on the fire at the same time.

"Halt!" I said. "Remove everything from the fire."

"Why?" she answered as this new interest crossed her mental threshold.

"What," I demanded, "are you intending to do to that steak?"

"It's none of your business," she retorted spiritedly.

"But it is," I insisted. "No man lives by bread alone, but bread—in the figurative sense for food—is one of the reasons for my coming here. So I repeat, what are you going to do to that steak—start its last earthly journey in a cold frying pan?"

She took alarm at this. Anyway, she also, in other ways, was a timid little thing.

"What do you suggest, maestro?" she asked, trying to appear at ease.

"I am still speaking of food," said I, keeping on the subject. "You've been to school. You have read a book. There are two important subjects you should have learned—physics and chemistry."

"But they're all concerned with making evil smells in a laboratory," she cried.

"Much better that," I said, "than later in life making evil tastes in the kitchen. Cooking," I went on, "is a simple process of changing the physical and chemical character of certain foods by exposing them to the action of heat.

"For example, take steak," I said. "What is steak?"

"Beef," she answered me simply.

"Not necessarily," I told her. "Steak can be veal, ham, venison, almost any large animal. Even whales produce steak of a sort. The English like it because the Government tells them to. But beefsteak comes from beef, as you stated. Reduced to scientific language, it is protein. It's like the white of egg. Expose it to heat and it coagulates, shrinks. So you sear your steak first to make the protein coagulate. That will keep the glucose, the moisture, the fat, the minerals and the hemoglobin inside where you want them. At least, where I want them."

"But you must add fat to the pan," she cried.

"I do hate to hear butter called fat," I observed. "But of course it's an appropriate term for that tasteless oil you have before you. Butter is fat, however," I added hastily.

"When do we start?" she asked me.

"We start cooking immediately. Have you any black market butter?"

Having secured my butter, I put it in the pan and let it melt until it began to turn brown and smoke slightly.

"That," I observed, "although melted, is still butter. But in another moment the heat will turn it into acrolein, which smells like an exhaust pipe. So in goes the steak while the butter is very, very hot but not too hot."

She watched transfixed as I seared the glorious mass of protein on each side until it had that blackish-brown look.

"Now," I said, thinking of future tête-à-têtes, "we turn down the fire slightly."

"Silly," she said after a pause, "you are just like a man. Why didn't you put salt on it before you started?"

"Salt," I said, "has a peculiar quality of calling unto itself all the moisture that is in its environment. That explains why you can never pour salt from a restaurant shaker. It has absorbed all the moisture from the circumambient atmosphere. How much more, then," I went on, "will it absorb from any substance with which it is in contact. Put salt on this steak and the salt will promptly call out the moisture both from the outside and the inside of that steak, leaving it sucked clean of all those delightful qualities which make a beefsteak most desirable."

"Why does that little bit of fat keep it from burning?" she asked me, seeing that the conversation couldn't be shifted from the subject of food for the time being.

"Why does a little bit of fat keep you from burning when you are toasting your altogether delightful shoulders on the beach at Bondi?" I answered. "Because fat is an insulator. While the steak has a coating of fat, it won't burn unless the fat burns. That's why you baste a chicken with fat when you are roasting it in the oven. Maybe we could find a chicken tomorrow."

She was impressed, so I continued.

"Since I want to do everything to make a more perfect wife of you, please note the happy ending to our chef d'oeuvre. Our steak is warming up rapidly inside as the heat penetrates, naturally enough, from the outside. This heat is turning the meat juices—the water—into steam. The steam is beginning to force its way out, even through the seared surface. When you see a little internal moisture sweating out —please excuse my coarseness—on the surface, the steak is ready.

"As a matter of record," I continued, "if you grill a lamb chop instead of frying it, the steam will blow it up until it is nearly round. And a pretty sight, too, a properly grilled lamb chop."

While I was explaining these things, I took out my steak and put on salt, pepper and a lump of butter. Then I added a bit of butter and a little water to the frying pan and quickly made an aromatic sauce to pour beside the steak. It was just a little water, but it does help the butter get the roasted flavorful juices off the frying pan.

We started to eat as I was pointing out what not to do in the way of cooking.

Said I, "If you start with a low fire, the outside won't coagulate and the liquids will run out and boil away. The steak will look grey and it will be flabby instead of firm and blackish-brown and aromatic."

The rest was silence. Unlike the mother of Tristram Shandy, I don't care for conversation during a sacrifice.

Soup in the Sun

There is a watercolor of Douglas Annand's which pictures a soft-curving green hill at Burradoo. Halfway up the hill are three big willow trees grouped about a white riding ring. Circling around inside the ring are the Southdown ponies on which gaily clad youngsters are learning to ride.

Doug painted this picture from the verandah of my cottage at Burradoo whilst his son was taking his first riding lessons. It was this happy picture that quickly came to mind when somebody once asked me what was my favorite dish?

"Onion Soup," I replied (thanks to the association of ideas), because so many of us have enjoyed this rich and golden soup from France sitting around the long wooden table on the verandah at Burradoo.

It is a beautiful place to be, especially on a sunny winter's day, with a plate of that wonderful soup in front of you, and a fragrant pine windbreak just a few yards away giving shelter from any cold little Westerly that might be wandering around trying to cool things.

Onion soup is more than a soup. It is a main course in its own right, and needs to be followed only by a cheese and a salad worthy of it, and perhaps a light sweet, to provide a completely satisfying meal.

FRENCH ONION SOUP

You can use chicken stock as a base or a stock made with boiling beef. The four French wives so often quoted in this book, and who provide many of the recipes, always use a chicken, but when I make it for my own pleasure, it's beef that goes into the stock pot.

So, taking either a fowl or four pounds of boiling beef, we add a small bunch of celery, a carrot and two onions cut in halves. Cut only the wilted leaves from the celery and don't chop up the vegetables into little pieces. We are going to simmer this stock very slowly so there will be plenty of time for all the flavor of the vegetables to be extracted. By keeping your vegetables in big pieces, they don't get mushy and so "cloud" the stock. Add three quarts of water, salt and pepper, and simmer for four hours.

Strain the stock, throw away the vegetables, and if you've used a boiling fowl, put it aside for some other family use.

Now, ever so gently, fry a pound and a half of sliced onions in butter. Whip out any piece that catches the least burn because we must preserve the golden color of the soup, which in this case is a very definite indication of its flavor.

When the onions are soft and golden from the butter, drop them into the stock which you have transferred to a fresh pot, taste for salt and pepper, and simmer for one hour.

Now take a baking dish or, better still, one of those extra-big enamel dishes of the sort that rice puddings are always made in. Line the bottom with very thin slices of golden toast, thin as Melba toast, and free of burns of course, and thickly cover with a good quarter inch of grated cheese. Pour the soup gently into the baking dish so that the cheese-loaded toast floats to the surface with as little disturbance as possible. Then another good, heavy layer of grated cheese on the now-floating toast, and into a medium oven for ten minutes so that cheese and toast merge into a light and creamy crust.

Take the baking dish straight to the table and serve.

CREME VICHYSSOISE

...AND ANOTHER LUNCHEON IN THE SUN

The great Louis Diat, chief chef of the Ritz-Carlton in New York for so many years, is the creator of this exquisitely smooth and creamy potato soup which is best served icy cold.

With this soup, too, we enjoy our memories of eating it in the sun.

In the spring of 1949 Deke and Louise Coleman returned from abroad. At that time I was living in the old stone coach house at 21 Gladswood Gardens. It is one of the most attractive little houses in Sydney, with Juliet balconies and wide French doorways opening onto a small lawn. At the far side of the lawn is a grey stone wall that drops, steep as a cliff, into Double Bay.

When people walked through the house and stepped out into the garden, it was about even money they would breathe, "This could be the coast of Cornwall" or "Just like the South of France!"

So the "welcome home" luncheon party for Deke and Louise was arranged on the lawn. But the balmy spring morning got hotter and hotter and it was only because the next-door fence grew a big enough one o'clock shadow that we were able to stay outdoors.

The menu consisted of Vichyssoise, roast chicken with rice, French salad and a sweet I've forgotten. But it was the iced Vichyssoise that was the great success on that warm day.

THE RECIPE

We will have to strain and re-strain this soup, so we start by cutting up the white part of four leeks very fine. Mince one onion very fine. Melt a quarter cup of butter in a heavy saucepan and cook the leeks and onions in this over a low flame until they are tender, but not brown. Add one quart of chicken stock (see chapter "Juice from the Chicken"), a tablespoon of chopped parsley, one stalk of celery, two potatoes sliced so thin they are almost transparent, salt and pepper. Simmer until the potatoes are tender. Now you put everything through your finest sieve. As Vichyssoise must be as smooth as cream, sieve it twice. For the second run through I use a coffee strainer. Correct your seasoning and put the soup in the tureen from which you're going to serve it, then put the tureen into your refrigerator for at least two hours. It's even worth while to chill the soup plates. Before serving, stir in a half pint of chilled cream.

Important! Use medium-sized leeks and potatoes; otherwise the Vichyssoise becomes so thick that the refrigerator might turn it to jelly.

On the table—or buffet—you will have a bowl of whipped cream and another of finely chopped chives. Let each guest float a little of each on top of their soup, and the more they know food, the more they will shower you with praise.

Philosophy of Frying

HEAT PEAKS OF BUTTER, OIL, WATER AND DRIPPING
AND THEIR EFFECTS ON FOOD

The wife of the minstrel boy got hold of me. Figuratively, of course. She said,

"Why can't I make French fried potatoes?"

I said, "Do you want to know, or is that just a lead in?"

Before she could answer, I went on. It's the only way to be a professor of anything.

"The rules," said I, "are the same as for any frying in deep fat. In point of fact, the French recognize only that method as frying.

"The difference between a pan full of water and pan full of oil is twofold. In the first place, oil is a better conductor of heat than water. That is one reason why it burns you so much more quickly and definitely than water when it splashes on you. In the second place, water, except in a pressure cooker, will not get any hotter than 212° F. Butter will reach 260° F. without decomposing, beef dripping can get as high as 370° F., and some of the vegetable fats like olive and peanut oil up to 450° F. If they get any hotter, they break down into a black, horrible-smelling substance. You can tell when they are just hot enough by two things. In the first place they begin to turn a spotty brown, and in the second place, to smoke. That's when you start.

The first rule to learn is that you must not put into the fat anything that is not dry on the surface. If there is a trace of water, the oil will spatter up in your face. The water vapor will form a thin layer on the outside of the potato or whatever you are frying. Because water is a poor conductor of heat, the heat from the oil won't penetrate and the potato will merely get mushy and anemic in color.

"While we are on the subject, what about those foods which cannot be wiped dry? Fish, for example. You can never wipe a fish dry because the mucus on his body makes him always a bit too damp.

"With the fish, then, we just use a lot of bread crumbs if we are in a hurry, or a mixture of flour, eggs, and water if we are not. We roll the fish in the chosen mixture so that his moisture doesn't come in contact with the hot oil. If we want to make a coating for the fish that won't absorb the taste of the cooking oil, we just add some melted butter or one of the tasteless vegetable oils to the paste before we roll our fish in it.

"One thing to remember," said I, "is that when you put a fish or potato into hot oil, it can only get hot in proportion to the heat it takes away from the oil. If it takes away the heat faster than the fire adds heat, you may find that you are trying to cook in oil which is not hot enough to do a good job. So you had better not put too much of anything into your oil at any one time.

"You can even cook fruit this way. They do in Italy."

"I learn from this," the lady broke in, "that cooking is merely a matter of transferring heat from air, water or oil to some food we want to change. And we suit the kind of heat to the kind of result we want. Right?"

"That is the principle. Now all you have to do is to practice. And fry your potatoes ten times this way before you invite me again . . . at least to eat."

"Just Give Me Plain Home Cooking"

MOLNAR

WHICH SHOULD BE A WARNING TO BACHELORS!

When the French use wine in cooking, it is always with discretion. The wine is added to coax out the richness in fowl or meat, or to give a sharp accent to the sauce for a fish. It is never there in its own right.

After all, in good cooking we seek the taste behind the taste. So!... if our taste buds are being soaked with cooked claret at every mouthful, how can they be expected to do very much savoring of shy but well-worth-seeking undertones of flavor?

Perhaps it's in the enthusiastic belief that the French use

wine in cooking as prodigally as the English use water that so many of our cooks, particularly the amateur male who is making his start at the stove, always give their dishes an overdose of wine. The chances are our cook is just as generous with garlic.

Garlic is all very well in its way. The Italians adore it. The French keep it in its proper place.

But our would-be Escoffier often rushes in—as I did when I started—with a bottle of wine in one hand and a clove of garlic in the other, and he's likely to use both far more liberally than his recipes require.

So, in applying ourselves to French cooking, we must remember that many of the tastiest dishes are the simplest. Let's take a beef casserole that keeps wine in its proper place as an undertone of flavor. The recipe comes from Mike Duval, who can seal as much flavor in a casserole dish as anyone I know.

BEEF CASSEROLE

Buy two pounds of top or bottom round steak. Choose the thickest slices. There's no need to buy filet or sirloin because we are going to marinate this steak for three hours before cooking. Most cheap cuts have more flavor than the tender ones, anyway.

Remove all the fat and cut the steak into pieces about four inches square. Pack them into a casserole dish with three sliced onions and two medium-sized carrots cut into one-half inch slices. (Keep your slices of vegetables even in thickness—then you get an even result in cooking. No big undercooked pieces or mushy little wisps.) Add salt and pepper. Also a small bouquet garni of thyme, marjoram and two bay leaves.

Now take hold of your bottle of wine and pour about a

cup and a half into the casserole dish. The wine barely covers the meat and vegetables. We assume there aren't any great open spaces around the meat or underneath it.

Cover and let stand for three hours. The meat will soak up the richness of the wine in the course of being tenderized.

When the time comes for cooking, put one tablespoon of butter into a frying pan. Lift your meat from casserole. Drain. By this time the butter should be sizzling. Quickly brown the meat on each side, sealing its juices.

Meantime you have removed the bouquet garni and popped the casserole with its wine, onions and carrots into a hot oven. By the time the meat is seared, the wine will be warm enough to receive it. Put your meat back into the casserole, together with the gravy it made in the pan, and add some small, whole onions and a stick or two of celery cut into three-inch slices.

As soon as the juice in the casserole is gently simmering, adjust the oven temperature to 350° F. and cook for two hours. If you haven't an oven thermometer—it's easy enough to buy one—just remember that the fluid in the casserole should never raise more than a gentle bubble. Also, the meat and vegetables at the top should be kept moist. Spoon the juice over them every now and then if necessary, but don't lift the lid more than you have to.

After the casserole has been in the oven for an hour and a half, add small, whole tomatoes which have been peeled. Scald in hot water to speed up peeling.

Thicken just before taking from oven. The best thickening is made with a quarter cup of the gravy taken from the oven mixed with one half tablespoon cornstarch.

This casserole is even better if made twenty-four hours beforehand. In this case, cook for one and a half hours, then turn off gas and leave casserole in oven. Next evening reheat, and wait until then to add tomatoes and thicken.

With any casserole you must have a foam of mashed potatoes to soak up the gravy.

ON THE MASHING OF POTATOES

Those of us who have any regard for potatoes will never mash them early to save the last-minute rush when the time comes to serve dinner. Adding extra milk to keep them moist only makes them gluey.

With a casserole, which is so simple to serve, we can afford to wait until the last minute before mashing. Depend upon butter, and plenty of whipping, to get that fluffy creaminess which makes mashed potatoes so much better than bread for mopping up rich gravy. Be restrained with the milk.

If mashed potatoes are a favorite weakness, and you want to taste them richer and lighter than you've ever known them before, add the yolk of an egg. As soon as you've broken up the potatoes, break in the egg. Whip like the dickens before you start adding butter and just a little milk.

A sprinkling of finely chopped chives adds flavor as well as appetizing color.

Three Cinderellas

Rounding off the previous chapter suggested the subject for this one—potatoes. We also offer a tasty little collection of recipes to increase respect for those other Cinderellas of the kitchen—the cabbage and the onion.

In the previous cookbook which Deke and I produced, the gentleman of Paris who supplied us with the recipes wept for the way in which the tender little pea is so often ill-treated. But nowhere did William Wallace Irwin give even a passing importance to the potato.

Recently it's been in short supply in many parts of this country because of shipping and pegged price. (Imagine the surprise in its eyes to find itself on the black market!) But we don't see it being treated any more kindly even when it costs its weight in artichokes.

Of course a well-baked potato with the Sunday roast, crisp and golden on the outside and floury within, is a tasty vegetable.

But so many things can be done to make a potato outstandingly good to eat, especially with grills. Let's discuss them before we continue with more French home cooking.

What are we writing! Treating the potato with full respect is very definitely French cooking.

Potatoes into Pommes-de-terre

NEW POTATOES – SMALL ONES SERVED IN BUTTER

Have you ever eaten new potatoes so small that they are no more than just marbles? It's worth while growing them yourself so that you can take them from the earth while they're still so very tiny it seems cruel. However, since the fruit shop man, as well as most of his customers, despises as runts these baby apples of the earth, you mightn't find it so very difficult to get them.

There's no waste with baby new potatoes because we keep the skin. Even if you can't get them marble size, any smallish new potatoes can be cooked like this.

Scrub with a stiff brush. Rinse. Boil about ten to fifteen minutes in salted water—a gentle prod with your fork will tell you when to drain off the water. After draining, hold the saucepan above the gas for no more than a second or so to steam off any surplus water and then drop in some lumps of butter and lower the saucepan down onto a less-than-medium gas. Sprinkle pepper on them at this stage. Keep shaking so that the hot butter slides all over each little spud and soaks well in. Put them, piping hot, beside your grilled steak, and write us and tell us how you like them . . . Here's another way.

POMMES-DE-TERRE A LA MAITRE D'HOTEL

Scrub the potatoes and, still in their skins which give off so much extra flavor, boil in salted water until tender.

Drain, peel and slice them one-eighth inch thick. Melt enough butter to take care of the amount of potatoes you're cooking—about one-fourth pound to one pound potatoes—and add two tablespoons of chopped parsley. Season with salt and pepper at this stage. Put the potatoes in this sauce and stir gently so that the butter covers all the slices. Serve very hot.

DUCHESSE POTATOES

Boil two pounds of peeled potatoes. Drain. Dry mash them enough to break up well. Add the yolks of three eggs—mashing between each yolk. Add just enough butter to bring them to a frothy creaminess. Add salt and a little pepper. Do not use milk, as we do not want sogginess. Now, between the palms of your hands roll the mashed potato, quickly and lightly, into small balls—each one about three-fourths inch in diameter. Roll lightly in flour.

Place in the refrigerator or some cool place for two hours. We've even prepared them this way the night before.

Five minutes before you're ready to serve, drop them into very hot, "deep fat." But make sure your "deep fat" is not so hot that it smokes. It's better to split them into two batches for this final cooking rather than crowd the saucepan. We've a very good reason for this advice, because when the small balls of potato are dropped into the deep fat they plummet straight to the bottom. But after a couple of minutes you'll see one float, light as Esther Williams, to the surface. Then another, and another, and another, until they're all pushing each other about on top looking for swimming room. So you can appreciate why the saucepan must not be crowded. As soon as they're a rich, golden brown all over, lift from the saucepan and drain on brown paper.

The word "fat" in "deep fat" does not necessarily mean fat, although you can use it if you must. Unless otherwise stated, "deep fat" is a generally used term signifying the use of any vegetable oil. By "deep" we mean a depth of at least three inches of bubbling hot oil.

POTATOES ANNA

These look like an upside-down cake, crisp and glistening, when they go to the table to be served. We'd never dream of cutting into them in the kitchen where there'd be no applause.

We start off by slicing the potatoes very fine. Very, very fine. You'll need enough slices to fill six cups. After a soaking in cold water, drain and dry with a towel. Then follow a good sprinkle of salt and a circle or two with the pepper mill.

Now take a round mould (the one we use is about two and a half inches deep by eight inches in diameter) and butter it well. Line it, sides and bottom, with your biggest slices. Then you fill in between these walls with layer upon layer of sliced potatoes, and between each layer you spread a tablespoon of butter. A final spread of butter all over the top. Bake in a hot oven (450° F.) for forty-five minutes. It might be well to take a peek at them after forty minutes, and a gentle prod right into the heart of Anna will tell if her potatoes are cooked. Turn out onto a warmed plate, being careful to keep the moulded shape which should be golden brown.

When serving with steak or thick slices of roast beef, you can encircle the mould of Potatoes Anna with fresh or fried parsley. Or you can form the ring with fried whole mushrooms.

SOUFFLEED POTATOES

These always seemed like the Indian Rope Trick. A few people claimed to have seen and, what's more, eaten them. But none seemed to know the trick of making a slice of potato puff itself up and huff itself up, and leave a great hollow space inside.

One day, browsing through a grand old-timer amongst recipe books, we came upon the recipe for potato puffs. No wonder they had eluded us for so long. They had been grandly christened as Soufflée!

The trick, and probably we'll find that the Indian Rope Trick is just as simple when we finally stumble upon it, lies in keeping two saucepans of fat, heated at different temperatures, beside each other. You'll also need a cooking thermometer. Personally we think this whole procedure something of a bother. But perhaps you were also born under the sign of Leo and don't mind a little bother if it gives you the opportunity to show what you can do.

Peel your potatoes. Cut in even slices one-eighth inch thick. It's important that the slices be even for perfect puffs. Put aside the little trimmings for some other use.

While we are about it, we might as well take out a biscuit cutter and make uniform discs, which add no end to the final impression on the visitors.

Soak the potato discs in iced water for fifteen minutes. Drain and dry thoroughly between towels.

Now, have you got those two saucepans of fat ready? One at 250° F., the other at 425° F. Fry your discs, a few at a time, in the 250° F. saucepan for three minutes. Keep them submerged and turn at least once. Precisely at the end of those three minutes lift them, in a wire basket, and put them straight into the 425° F. saucepan. PUFF! Up they come without any waiting. Keep them there until they're lightly browned.

Now in a medium oven, about 350° F., you've spread a piece of brown paper on a baking dish or iron tray. Drain your puffs on this paper. Salt and serve as soon as you can—straight from oven.

Onions

If onions grew for onion soup alone they would be well worth all the tears that they have caused us. But their blessings are many and their lusty peasant breath, which quickly changes so much for the better in the cookpot, is always full of promise. On a cold winter's night, as we wait for the lift on the 11th floor of our office building, we sometimes smell onions frying with steak in our caretaker's flat. That rich, good smell of a family meal is as cozy as anything in Dickens, and cheers us up on our homeward way.

ONIONS TO SERVE WITH CORNED BEEF

Peel and drop into boiling water for five minutes. Drain. This pre-boiling deprives them of their coarse smell. Now into boiling salted water and cook until they're soft but not broken. Drain. Back into a saucepan. Put a small dab of butter on each onion, followed by one-half tablespoon of cream. Season with salt and pepper. Simmer with lid on for five minutes, taking great care not to burn.

FRENCH FRIED ONIONS

Use large onions. Cut in slices one-fourth inch thick and separate each slice into rings. If you're pressed for time, just dip the rings in milk, drain and dip in flour. Fry in deep fat, drain on brown paper and sprinkle with salt.

We know another way that needs more time but not much more effort. First make a batter by sifting two cups of flour with a teaspoon of salt. (This quantity is enough for eight people and generous for six.) Add one cup of milk, three well-beaten eggs and two tablespoons of butter. Mix well and let stand in refrigerator.

Slice four big onions and separate into one-eighth inch rings. Soak in milk for two hours. Then be sure and drain them very well. Dip them into the batter one at a time and drop them into hot deep fat. These, as with the Pommes-de-terre Duchesse, will soon swim to the surface and breast stroke around as they brown. Correct seasoning as they drain.

We have two other favorite recipes for onions but, as they provide for serving onions as quite a dish in their own right, you will find them in other chapters. Under "Soup in the Sun" you will find Onion Soup, which of all foods is one of our great favorites. Under "Cocktails to Cockcrow" you will find "Onion Tart."

Cabbage

Boiled cabbage has a depressing smell and you must tell those people in the flat next door that there's a preparation now being sold in a little bottle with a wick in it. Tell them that all they need do when they're boiling cabbage is to uncork the bottle, expose the wick to the air and, presto, the smell of cooking cabbage disappears, leaving the kitchen air country fresh.

Having disposed of the Philistines, let us demonstrate to them how a cabbage should be cooked.

Every cabbage comes to us with almost enough moisture in its leaves to take care of its cooking. Even a walloping big cabbage requires hardly more than a cup of water and the lid clamped down tight.

STEAMED CABBAGE

Select a small, firm cabbage. It's better to buy two small ones rather than one large one, because the small ones have so many more of those crisp, juicy and almost-white leaves. Shred coarsely. One-fourth inch to one-half inch strips. Soak in water for twenty minutes. Drain. At this stage even a small cabbage will carry almost all the water it requires. No more than a tablespoonful of water need be added for the cooking. Also add a tablespoonful of lemon juice, some salt, and clamp the lid on tight. Cook slowly for about twenty minutes. Serve while still firm.

We wouldn't open a bottle of white wine especially for the purpose, but if you've got a drop in the bottle from the night before, or like to borrow a little from the bottle you're serving for dinner, you can substitute it for part or whole of the water. In which case you will use less lemon juice.

Or you can take your cabbage steamed in water and lemon juice a step further with cream.

After draining thoroughly and testing for seasoning, put back in saucepan and quickly reheat, holding high over flame. Pour enough cream over cabbage to cloak, but not soak, all shreds. Shake over flame to send cream well through the shreds, and serve as soon as possible.

Five Courses
for Confucius

A COMPLETE CHINESE DINNER WITH A LITTLE
FOOD FOR THOUGHT

Only the toss of a double-headed penny could decide whether Karl Marx or Confucius has been most quoted by people who have never read a word either gentleman wrote.

Every Sunday afternoon for years and years Karl had had to look down from whatever spot in heaven philosophers go to, and hear his name taken in vain by his soapbox disciples. Much damage has been caused as a result.

There is Confucius sitting beside him playing on his harp, on which we know he was an expert back in China over 2,000 years ago

Says Confucius, pausing between celestial notes, and smiling benignly on Karl, "When a country is in order, it is a shame to be a poor and common man. When a country is in chaos, it is a shame to be rich and an official." Leaving Karl to ponder that one, he continues with his playing.

Confucius wished for a better world, just as Karl Marx did, and that wish guided all he wrote. But, as a man who enjoyed good food as well as philosophy, he has never been in danger of setting his fellow men against each other.

Next to the food of France must surely come the food of China. Light, delicate and easily digested, it is, so far as we have explored it, appetizing to look at and delicious in flavor.

Practically every Chinese restaurant of any reputation in Sydney, and some in Melbourne, has been patronized by your authors. One of us is more enthusiastic than the other who, having ventured and approved, nevertheless insists that as French cooking is the better of the two, he will remain with it.

But the other of us (the one without a French wife) is more catholic in taste and has collected a number of Chinese recipes. He has sniffed his way into Chinese kitchens, asked many questions, and poked about in the meat and vegetable shops of Campbell Street, where a European customer is still a novelty.

The years have passed and with their passing has come some success with the cooking of the simpler Chinese dishes. About half a dozen have become firm favorites whether we eat out in Chinese restaurants or cook them ourselves, and here they are.

As individual courses, each is ample for eight, with the exception of the Spring Rolls, where the quantities are enough for four to six rolls, depending upon the size of your pancakes.

In a final full-dress rehearsal for this chapter, I served this dinner buffet-style to twelve people. Quantities for the chicken, pork and fish were exactly as given here and quite sufficient in view of the fact that I was serving five courses. However, I doubled the quantity of Spring Rolls and used ten cups of cooked rice for the Fried Rice, the balance of the ingredients in proportion.

FRIED RICE (MA CHOW FON)

Fried rice is an absolute must with any Chinese dinner.

As with practically every Chinese dish, it's simple enough and mostly a matter of chop, chop, chop right until the last minute when you throw everything together in the pot, after which the cooking is soon over. So let us start our preparation.

1. Fry 2 eggs until the yolks are firm. Cool them off on grease-proof paper and when they're cool, slice them into ¼″-wide strips.
2. Shell a pound of shrimp, and if they're big ones, clean them and break them in two.
3. Peel and slice ¼ pound of mushrooms. (Can be left out, but we like them.)
4. Finely dice ½ cup of onions.
5. Chop up a chicken leg into pieces about 1″ square. This can be filched from the chicken you've bought for the chicken and almonds, if you're preparing a full Chinese dinner.
6. Chop up a tablespoonful of cooked ham or fried bacon.
7. Cut 3 shallots or scallions, leaving a little of the green for color, into ½″ lengths.

With all this shelling and chopping out of the way, we start the actual frying. This is so simple that I usually fry

my rice over a flame burner at the table just before the other dishes are brought in. It makes quite an impression. But first you have to get your flame burner and, at the risk of never being given another good table, I'll tell you that it was Pierre at Princes who had one made for me.

8. Heat 2 tablespoons of vegetable oil in a frying pan. Keep flame at a moderate heat all of the time you're frying. When the oil is really hot but not yet smoking . . .

9. . . . add egg strips, shrimp, mushrooms, ham and onion. Don't leave them for more than ½ a minute at a time. Keep stirring. After 5 minutes . . .

10. . . . Add 4 cups of cooked rice that has been well drained. Toss in the chopped shallots or scallions at the same time. Mix other ingredients through the rice as you stir, being careful not to break them up or let them get mushy.

At this stage it is better to find that you have used too little oil instead of too much and, as the pan is now very hot, another drop or two of oil may be added.

It takes only a few minutes to heat the rice right through, and your fried rice is then ready to serve.

There is one thing you must keep in mind. Your boiled rice must not be gluey before it goes into the frying pan. Up goes the wail, "But how can you boil rice without it all sticking together?" For that we have the answer.

HOW TO BOIL RICE WITHOUT MAKING GLUE

If you have eaten in a Chinese home or restaurant, you will have noted that a Chinese chef does not cook his rice as long as we do. You almost say that he comes close to undercooking his rice. The grains have no desire to stick together because each grain, although cooked right through, is still firm. Start to hover over your rice a few minutes before the cooking time is up. Just a minute or two can turn what was perfectly boiled rice into a gluey mush.

The following method is almost a process of steaming instead of boiling.

1. Wash rice thoroughly.
2. For each cup of rice use 1½ cups of cold water.
3. Bring rice to a boil over a good, moderate flame. Give it a minute of this boiling, then ...
4. ... Turn gas down very low, slide an asbestos mat under the saucepan and leave it for 15 minutes before lifting the lid but giving saucepan an occasional shake to keep rice from sticking to bottom. If your gas flame has been just right, which doesn't always happen, there should be hardly a drop of water in the saucepan after the 15 minutes is up and the rice should be firm and floury right through. Make a quick test by tasting before you ...
5. ... Drain off surplus water. Shake rice well. Drain again.

Paulette Pellier once gave me a helpful tip for rice that has been allowed to get too "wet," and it is also something to be remembered for keeping even properly cooked rice warm and nicely separate. Spread your rice out in a baking dish. Scatter little peas of butter all over it. Put in a warm oven.

CHICKEN AND ALMONDS

These quantities are for a chicken of 2 lbs. to 3½ lbs. in weight. The chicken should be steamed in an ordinary saucepan or cooked in a pressure cooker until tender.

You will have to boil up the bones after you take the meat off them, because you'll need a cup of chicken stock.

1. Steam the chicken. When cooked, separate from bone. Cut the chicken meat into 1½" squares.
2. Cut 3 celery stalks into 1" pieces.
3. Slice ¼ lb. mushrooms into 1" squares, but leave the small mushrooms whole.
4. Fry ½ cup of shelled almonds in oil or butter until they are golden and starting to go brown on the tips.
5. There's a vegetable called Chinese cabbage which looks something like spinach. It's sometimes seen in suburban greengrocers. If you're putting on a full Chinese dinner, it's worth going to the Chinese quarter of the city where you'll soon find a "butcher's" shop which also sells vegetables. There you will certainly come upon your Chinese cabbage (and also chunky cuts of pork that are perfect for sweet-and-sour pork). Chinese cabbage is not indispensable, but if you can obtain it, cut up a cupful, using much more stalk than leaf, into 1" squares.

We commence cooking.

1. Heat 2 tablespoons of vegetable oil in a frying pan (with lid) or saucepan. When the oil is thoroughly hot, add chicken, mushrooms, celery, Chinese cabbage. Stir lightly until they've taken up the heat—about 2 minutes. Add about 1¾ cups chicken stock. Put on lid and keep over that moderate flame for about 5 minutes. Thicken with a tablespoon of cornstarch mixed with chicken stock. Keep stirring while the juice is thickening.
2. Give the chicken a few more minutes and serve piping hot. The vegetables will look part-cooked by European standards, but taste the extra flavor in them!

SWEET-AND-SOUR PORK

1. Crush 1 small clove of garlic.
2. Cut 2 large green peppers into 8 pieces, after taking out the hot core and seeds. Boil peppers until almost tender—about 6 minutes. Drain. Set aside.
3. You'll need to be ready with a cup of chicken stock.
4. Take 4 slices of canned pineapple or fresh pineapple that has been simmered for 5 minutes in a syrup composed of 1 cup of water to ½ cup of sugar. Cut each thick slice into 4 pieces.
5. Cut 2 to 3 lbs. of lean pork into 1″ cubes.
6. Make a batter by beating together 2 eggs with 4 tablespoons of flour, 1 teaspoon of salt and a dash of pepper.
7. Drop the pork into this batter and mix around.
8. Heat ¾ cup of vegetable oil in a heavy pan.
9. Drop in pork piece by piece. After 5 minutes the first little piece of pork should be golden brown on one side. Turn him over and, if he's right, continue with the rest.
10. When the pork is golden brown all over, drain off almost all of the oil, leaving what you judge to be about a tablespoonful in the pan. Actually, the pan and the pork are just about moist with hot oil and no more.
11. Add 2/3 cup of chicken stock, the pineapple and green peppers. Put lid on tightly and cook over a low flame for 10 minutes.
12. During the next 10 minutes stir together 1 tablespoon of cornflour, 4 teaspoons of soy sauce, 1 cup of vinegar, 1 cup of sugar and 1½ cups of chicken bouillon. This is your sweet-and-sour sauce. You'll soon learn it by heart if you do much Chinese cooking.

13. Add this sauce to your pan and stir it well through the pork and vegetables while the juice is thickening. After 5 minutes of simmering from the time you add the thickening, you can serve.

SWEET-AND-SOUR FISH

This dish is easy because if you include it in your Chinese dinner, you simply make an extra quantity of the sweet-and-sour sauce which you prepared for the pork in the previous recipe.

If you should raise your eyes at the suggestion that two dishes on the same menu should be served with the same sauce, let us reassure you that this is quite in order, as sweet-and-sour sauce is almost as basic in the cooking of China as beef stock or chicken stock is in the cooking of France.

1. Use a whole snapper. Clean, also remove the eyes, which you don't want to see reproaching you from the middle of a festive table.
2. Put a wire cake stand or any similar support into a covered baking dish with just enough water to lap

against the cross wires. Squeeze the juice of 2 lemons into this water.

3. Place snapper, complete with head and tail, onto the wire stand. Steam until tender but not falling apart.

4. Make your sweet-and-sour sauce. Here is the recipe again to save you looking back and working out certain slight adjustments. Stir together 1 tablespoon of cornstarch, 4 teaspoons of soy sauce, 1 cup of vinegar, 1 cup of sugar and 1½ cups of chicken stock. Heat this mixture over a moderate heat, with frequent stirring. When thoroughly hot, drop in 4 slices of canned pineapple cut into quarters together with 2 green peppers which have had their hot seeds removed, have been boiled until tender and cut into quarters. (I also add, as the Chinese do, thin slices of slightly boiled carrot to the sweet-and-sour sauce I serve with fish.) Keep over flame until pineapple, peppers and carrots take on the heat. If not ready to serve immediately, your sweet-and-sour sauce can be set aside and heated at the last minute.

5. Place snapper onto a heated dish. Fill the eye sockets with a couple of stuffed olives, which put quite a naughty look back into the old boy's eyes. Pour the steaming hot sweet-and-sour sauce all over your fish, and it goes to the table.

SPRING ROLLS

SOMETIMES CALLED EGG ROLLS

Ah! Spring Rolls! Those golden, crisp, crackling pancake cases bulging to the breaking point because they're over-stuffed with shrimp, shallots, egg, celery, ham and cabbage!

The pancake batter first. You'll notice that water is used instead of milk. You'll find that water makes it easier to get a thinner pancake.

1. Break 2 eggs. Beat slightly. Take away a tablespoon of this beaten egg and set aside in a cup to use later for sticking together the edges of the pancakes when you lap them over the filling to make the roll.
2. Twice sift ½ cup of flour into a bowl, adding a little extra flour if necessary at the second sifting to make up the half-cup measure.
3. Beat well together the beaten eggs, ½ cup of water, and a good pinch of salt.
4. Pour this mixture into the flour a little at a time, beating until thoroughly smooth and not the tiniest lump of flour remains.

As with any batter, this mixture can be made hours before, even days before, and is all the better for standing.

THE FILLING

1. Prepare ¼ cup of finely shredded cooked carrot, 1 cup of lightly cooked, finely sliced celery, and 1 cup of lightly cooked shredded cabbage. (Simmer all together for 5 minutes and then strain thoroughly.)
2. Add to these 3 finely chopped shallots or scallions, 1 tablespoon of cooked ham, ½ lb. of cooked, chopped shrimp, a good pinch of salt, a light sprinkle of sugar and a thimbleful of vegetable oil. Mix well together.

FRYING THE PANCAKES

As with Crepes Suzette, you heat your pan, which should be a small one about the size of a pancake, and put no more than a sliver of butter into it to make the surface greasy. The best way I can describe the right amount of buttering is to remind you of the greased plates you see sizzling in the window of any Hamburger Palace.

Pour a tablespoon of batter into the hot pan and lift immediately from the flame. Quickly jiggle pan backwards and forwards to help the batter spread evenly and thinly. A minute or less should see the underside cooked. Stop! You don't turn it over. The white-side-up becomes the inside of your spring roll. Place your first pancake on a warmed plate. Cook your next pancake, and so you start to pile them on top of each other.

ASSEMBLY LINE

Into the center of each pancake, with the white side up, remember, place as much of the mixture as you think it will

hold when folded over, because your Spring rolls must be plump.

Turn in the ends first and then roll the pancakes over the filling, using that beaten egg you put aside earlier to stick the edges together.

All this can be done hours before you serve dinner, because the rolls are to be set aside in the refrigerator until you are ready to fry them.

THE FRYING

Fill your frying pan almost to the height of your rolls with vegetable oil. When the oil is hot, put in your rolls but don't crowd them. Cook until golden brown on one side. Turn and cook until golden brown on the other.

There, at long last, is the recipe for which many have pleaded but few have been given because one day we knew we would get around to writing our cookbook.

These five recipes provide a well-rounded Chinese dinner. They are all quite easy, but we respectfully suggest that you try them one at a time. Not that these recipes are difficult. But, with all the chopping of ingredients for five courses, you must have the experience needed for a clear plan of action.

SEASONING OF CHINESE DISHES

The Chinese use soy sauce instead of salt and pepper for seasoning. Almost any better-class grocer now sells soy sauce, but we prefer to go to a Chinese grocery shop and buy a bottle with a label that unmistakably states that it is bottled in China.

A little soy sauce is poured over the food on the plate

just as you would use salt and pepper. An exception is any dish served with sweet-and-sour sauce. All of these dishes may be seasoned with a little salt if necessary before adding the sweet-and-sour sauce.

If you are without soy sauce you can season the food with salt and pepper while it is still in the saucepan.

SERVING THE DINNER

Chinese food cools quickly, so we always use bowls, because a bowl keeps food much hotter than a plate. As the chain stores are now selling Chinese individual bowls quite inexpensively, let us buy one for each guest. They can always double up as soup plates.

Set a bowl, on a plate, in front of each guest. Soy sauce has a habit of spilling, so the service plate is a real need. If you want to see what you can do with chopsticks, remember that for rice the bowl is held by the left hand close to the mouth and the right hand keeps the chopsticks busy.

The first course to come to the table is your large bowl of fried rice. The fried rice goes along with the courses just as bread does with a European dish. Bring the rest of the courses to the table as quickly as possible.

Each guest takes a helping of fried rice with a little soy sauce. Then he helps himself to a spoonful of one or two of the other courses as they take his fancy.

I try to get the chicken-with-almonds and the sweet-and-sour pork to the table right on the heels of the fried rice. Then the Spring Rolls. Finally, our olive-eyed snapper makes as grand an entrance as any leading baritone.

Observations on the Sense of Taste

... AND WHY OUR PALATES IMPROVE WITH AGE

Sir Francis Galton invented a small whistle adjustable to very high tones. His object was to find out what was the upper limit of hearing of humans. He was surprised to learn that the hearing of children was much more acute than their elders.

Children have a far more sensitive palate than their elders, as well as hearing. Because it is sensitive, they cannot bear to eat the things that their elders find most appetizing.

Dickens' orphans, in finding the meat floating in fat repulsive, were being normal children. Some adults like the taste of fat, but to many children a piece of pure fat is practically an emetic. It was not only Jack Spratt who could eat no fat. Few people can eat it until age has dulled the acuity of the taste buds.

The same is true for caviar, olives, Camembert, Gorgonzola, Limburger, pickled pork, and a great many vegetables including the much-detested spinach. Children are sensitive to sugar and can eat dishes that are an emetic to an adult. Parents who try to deprive their children of sweets and sweet drinks are as unnatural and foolish as the prohibitionist who tries to deprive adults of their alcohol. Incidentally, the child's palate is so sensitive that he cannot drink alcohol unless it is heavily sugared or watered.

No child becomes an expert wine or tea taster. He couldn't. His taste becomes specialized by becoming dulled. He can taste the overtones only when his taste ignores the central theme.

A Punch cartoon once showed a maid bringing in to her blimpish employer a pheasant that she was holding at arm's

length. She was saying, "Will that be high enough for master?" To a child, or a servant who has not become accustomed to the smell of high meat, it is offensive. But when the taste buds have been dulled, the taste of high meat is strong enough to get over the threshold of sensitivity. More delicate foods lose their savor as age advances simply because grandfather can no longer notice subtle nuances. His taste must be stimulated with a sledgehammer.

Obviously neither is wrong. If grandfather likes to sit by the fire while Junior plays cricket, that is a question of bodily needs. But in the question of food, elders have the authority, and they like to think that they have cultivated their sensitivity beyond that of the child. They like to lord it over the youngsters because they are in a position of authority. They notice that children prefer processed Cheddar to Gorgonzola, and they think that they are little savages for preferring it. But children cannot bear strong cheeses. They find the mild flavor of processed cheese just at the limit of their appreciation.

Some people with an acute sense of taste never learn to like adult foods. As Hamlet says, it remains to them as "caviar to the general." But it is also true that some people retain a very acute sense of hearing to a considerable age. The only general rule is that age does diminish sensitivity of all sorts.

Juice from the Chicken

Have you ever tasted young beans steamed in chicken stock and served hot, as a course on their own, with a large dab of butter melting all over them?

Have you ever boiled your rice for savory use in chicken stock instead of water?

A poached egg is a watery-looking thing, but next time you have to tempt either an invalid or your own appetite, poach an egg in the rich juice from the chicken and sprinkle the golden yolk with red paprika.

You'll baffle your guests over and over again by using chicken stock instead of water. For instance, the flavor of those beans which were served as a course on their own, had us puzzled for weeks after we ate them. At long last it was "my sister Evie" who hit upon the reason for their richness. Chicken stock.

Good cooks are always watching for such little wrinkles. Knowing them, we get more out of recipes than others do, and so are reputations made.

All very well. But have we no respect for money? What hope have we of using chicken stock as often as we'd like to use it, with tough old boilers selling at today's prices.

What we'd give to be able to cook on a farm (for ourselves, of course) where there is always an old rooster who has lost the respect of his harem!

Just one cup of chicken stock can make a world of difference to many a dish, and we don't have to live on a farm to be able to use chicken stock much more often.

Just think of all the chicken bones that you've tossed into the dustbin. There goes your chicken stock, and the moral is, never throw away the carcass of a chicken. The bones still have juice in them after cooking, especially if they've been cooked in a pressure cooker.

Save the bones that don't go onto the plates. Break them up with all those little pieces of meat that are still on them. Into a small pot with the lot, together with any giblets or claws that the poultryman might have been generous enough to leave attached to the bird. Add a big onion. Also a stick of celery if it's at hand. Pepper and salt. Cover with water, gently simmer, and you'll find yourself with a cup or two of rich chicken stock ready for the next recipe that asks for it.

CHICKEN CONSOMME SANS VERMOUTH

We're not above gathering up old bones for chicken stock, but for that exquisite essence of chicken, a limpid consommé, we'll travel by trolley instead of taxis and treat ourselves to a whole bird especially for this subtle soup.

As the bird has to be simmered very slowly, his flesh can be taken off his bones for a family curry on the following night.

Before taking you into the kitchen, we must denounce those head waiters who try to cover up for the lack of flavor in their consommé by making a great to-do of spilling a glass of French Vermouth or Sherry into the soup plate as it is placed before the diner.

The clearest consommé, and our consommé shall be the clearest of clear, must carry in its own liquid all the flavor with which it is going to entrance the palate.

To get so much natural flavor into an absolutely clear soup takes only time, a generously big bird, and fresh vegetables. Remove the little lumps of fat from inside the fowl and then put it into a pot that has a tight lid, and is just big enough to take it comfortably. Add cold water to cover. Add a good half bunch of celery, two whole onions and a medium-sized carrot that has been well scrubbed and cut into chunky one-inch pieces. Add a little salt. With so much celery, less salt seems to be required. Bring to a vigorous simmer, then turn the gas so low that it barely maintains the simmering. Every half hour or so wipe away the scum that collects around the side of the saucepan. Also watch out for any beads of grease on the surface and lift them out by dabbing a flat piece of brown paper against them. But you'll need to do this quickly because we mustn't keep the lid off the pot a second longer than we can help. Flavor escapes with the steam.

After five hours of gentle simmering, you will have extracted just about all of the flavor from the fowl and the vegetables. Lift them out and strain the broth through cheese cloth.

Reheat the broth, but not past the simmering point. Correct the seasoning, and there's your consommé. It's so clear you can see the gold crest on the bottom of your soup plate, and yet it has a most satisfying flavor.

Such a consommé stimulates the appetite for the course to follow, and leaves no doubt that an important dinner has begun.

Do we serve bread with this consommé? We do not! Instead, we make small puff pastry turnovers with a filling of chopped lettuce and egg.

PUFF PASTRY TURNOVERS FOR CONSOMME

Ready-made puff pastry can be extremely good, so we use it for these turnovers, rolling it out as thin as we dare. Cut it into triangles with five-inch sides. Now chop up two hard-boiled eggs fairly fine and shred eight lettuce leaves. Mix the egg and lettuce together. A sprinkle of salt and a good sprinkle of pepper. Put a fat pile of egg and lettuce into the center of each triangle and then fold the pastry over the filling, sealing the edges with beaten egg yolk. Also wipe some egg yolk across the top of each turnover for professional polish. These can be made hours ahead of time and kept in the refrigerator until you are ready to pop them into a hot oven. Ten minutes should be enough to see them rise and shine a golden brown.

Then onto the table they go—one beside each steaming plate of consommé.

On the Roasting of Chicken

Those of us who grew up with a love for the stuffing in chicken, turkey or even beef olives* will always have a nostalgia for it. Especially when we smell someone else's Sunday dinner cooking and know that all we have is a lonely piece of steak waiting for us at home.

But having grown up, and come under the influence of the French, our palate, we think, has improved.

When sage, marjoram and thyme get together with bread crumbs inside of a chicken, they're a strong combination. So strong, especially the sage, that the delicate flavor of our tender little chicken has to play second fiddle to them.

So let's enjoy our seasoning in beef olives (they cost less anyway) and next time roast the chicken this way . . . Rub salt and pepper all over the chicken and sprinkle a little more salt and pepper inside.

Melt a quarter pound or more of butter, depending on size of bird. Pour this all over chicken and place in 425° F. oven. Add two tablespoons of water to baking dish. Baste every few minutes for first fifteen minutes. Reduce oven to 350° F. and continue basting at close intervals until chicken is cooked.

Serve with its own sauce. When chicken is cooked, remove to warm plate. Place baking dish with its rich butter and chicken sauce on top of good, quick heat. As it sizzles, add two tablespoons of hot water. Stir together and pour over each serving of chicken. By special request—no flour.

* Small slices of meat seasoned, rolled up and cooked.

On the carving. Never again do we carve a chicken in slices, allowing the juice to run out. Cut and break chicken into four, six or eight pieces, according to size of bird and number of guests ... A wing goes with a fat piece of breast; a leg with a beautiful piece of plump thigh. Or just a large piece of breast, solid through from crisp skin to where the flesh leaves the bone.

Taking Liberties with Maryland

Far be it from us to try to improve on any of the great classical recipes.

Yet browsing from cookbook to cookbook we read wide differences in the recipes given for famous dishes.

In our kitchen library there are nine ways to make Beef Stroganoff, a choice of four batters for Crepes Suzette, two radically different instructions for Lobster Newburg. That's enough research to justify our particular variation of Chicken Maryland.

Now the chicken that often brings shame to the fair name of Maryland possibly is not Chicken Maryland at all. It's our bet that when the chicken comes from the pan too dry, then the chef has hit upon a recipe that no real Maryland cook would ever recognize.

Yet such frying can happen in Maryland, itself. We made a lunch-time pilgrimage there during a week-end visit to Washington. The restaurant specialized! Perhaps we should blame the chicken. There was too much crisp and not enough flesh.

To forestall such disaster, let us take our Chicken Maryland out of the frying pan and into the casserole.

It was "my sister Evie," Mrs. Hal Hulme, who developed this recipe to our liking some years back.

Deke and Louise were invited for dinner and, as usual, they were late.

To save the chicken from drying up in the pan—her cookbook instructed open-pan frying from start to finish— she transferred it to the casserole. When that chicken eventually reached the table, even though its batter was slithering off its limbs, it was still glistening with its own juices. And succulent! It was delicious chicken and that, with some very slight adjustments, is how we've had our Chicken Maryland ever since!

. . . Cut chicken into four, six or eight pieces according to size. Rub with salt and pepper. Rub with flour. Dip in egg. Then dip in bread crumbs. Fry in hot butter just long enough to brown each piece on all sides.

Remove from pan and pack into casserole. Pour butter from pan all over chicken. Add no other fluid. Put lid on tightly and cook in moderate oven until tender, or about one hour.

When casserole is opened there will be plenty of juice to pour over chicken before serving.

Chicken Maryland needs its traditional accompaniment of fried bananas and sweet corn fritters.

You know how to fry bananas, but once again Evie has a luscious way of her own with fritters, using sweet corn from the can.

SWEET CORN FRITTERS

Put one cup of corn into a bowl. Add one whole egg and two tablespoons of flour. Pepper and salt. Stir quickly and lightly together with a wooden spoon.

Put two tablespoons of butter into a heavy pan. When hot, drop in corn—a spoonful at a time. Wait until fritters are brown, then lift with pancake turner and brown on other side.

Important note on frying of these fritters: Once your heavy pan is hot enough to take them, the heat should then be reduced to the lowest possible flame and remain low so that they can take their time in browning. Remember, also, there is flour in them and they can do with the cooking.

MOLNAR

Interlude

There are more ways of spoiling a meal before it is started than there are of cooking it right.

People read a recipe in their favorite magazine and spontaneously invite someone to come over and try it. Nothing could be more certain of breaking a friendship. The greatest rule in friendship and in cooking is: Never invite a guest to eat a dish which you haven't prepared for yourself ten times before.

No recipe is absolute. Qualities of flour differ, meat is tougher or tenderer, the temperature cannot be guaranteed to be exactly the same throughout any two cookings. Vegetables differ between fresh and woody, potatoes are solid or floury. The same fruits have more or less sugar in them, or less juice and perfume. Any two collections of ingredients will differ within a wide range, unless they are taken out of cans produced by the same manufacturer at the same time and in the same place.

It does not matter how complete and accurate the recipe is. It does not matter how perfect the cooking controls via thermostats may be. It does not matter if the kitchen is as scientific as a laboratory. You cannot exclude the human element. To the science of cooking must be added the art of cooking. No human being ever learned anything completely from a book. You must get into the kitchen and do the job over many times before you have the feel of it.

When Doctor Johnson was "invited to dine, even with an intimate friend, he was not pleased if something better than a plain dinner was not prepared for him. I have heard him say on such an occasion, 'this was a good dinner enough, to be sure; but it was not a dinner to ask a man to.'"

The first thing a cook has to do is to make sure that the ingredients are absolutely right. Maybe you have a supplier who has everything at the peak of quality in season and out. If so, you might profitably be examined with a lie-detecting machine. Most cooks have to prowl around, feeling this and that (surreptitiously, if the shopman won't have it otherwise) and going from shop to shop to make sure that what they have is the top quality for that season and that day.

If you are economizing (and in a Grade A dinner don't try to) you had better let what is available at the market determine your menu, rather than to determine your menu and then go to market. Your meals in general will be better if you buy what is in abundance. Generally that means that the price is best, and it is the peak of the season. Don't buy old, withered vegetables at any price. They have lost their taste and their value in vitamins.

Don't forget that the sense of taste is more sensitive than science. People can detect delicate nuances in food and wine that completely escape the laboratory investigator. Strong things like cheese, melons, onions and (more frequently than ought to be permitted) coal oil, disinfectants and soap can be tasted even though they were at some distance from the food being prepared.

Some people like strong tastes. There are nationalities which specialize in them. I am not thinking of the Sicilian and his garlic at the moment, but of the Scots. The Scots—a stout people—will have nothing but sodium bicarb to raise their scones. The reason is simple. When sodium bicarb is heated, it gives off carbon dioxide and becomes sodium carbonate. The latter is better known as washing soda, and not as one of the more desirable condiments. It gives to the scones a faint taste of what soap would taste like if it hadn't been subjected to the process of saponification. But, as I said, the Scots are a stout people. They like haggis.

Simple, inexpensive dishes are very often the best. Speaking for myself, a supper made of really good noodles and butter is one of the most delicate things on earth. I often have that and a glass of milk when I am on my own. The taste is too delicate to stand up to the competition of wine. There are a thousand ways of serving noodles so as to modify their taste, but the evanescent flavor of good hard wheat with the subtle addition of butter is something hard to beat.

Incidentally, it would be possible to feed a large family very economically on such dishes. Butter is expensive, but not as expensive as meat and cakes. So use it to make inexpensive things taste expensive.

When you are eating by yourself, eat in the kitchen. Food never tastes as good as it does when it goes from the stove straight onto your plate. When you have to carve a big roast for eight people it is lukewarm when they get it. The volatile aromatics have disappeared, or have condensed and precipitated themselves on the dish. That delightful bouquet as you open the oven door is nothing other than appetite-provokers taking wing. There isn't much you can do about this when you have company, but you needn't do it when you are alone.

Beans at a Barbecue

MOLNAR

Every holiday cottage should have its barbecue. Not one of
those prissy, spick-and-span suburban barbecues of faced
brick with fancy scrolls, but a sprawling barbecue built of
rough-quarried stone with long arms stretching out on each
side on which you can pile dishes or drop sizzling-hot grillers
from suddenly burnt fingers. On such arms you can sit, as
the sun goes down and the Southern Cross comes up, and
wait for the gum logs to settle into glowing coals.

If the logs are slow in reducing, then pile great branches
of green gum leaves on them. They roar into quick flame,
hasten the coming of the coals, and give you a wonderful,
pungent fragrance to breathe in—a fragrance which goes
very well with beer.

In any case, as soon as the coals are properly glowing and ready, I throw onto them a bunch of gum tips. There remains just enough of a memory of them attached to the griller to add the very faintest taste of the bush to the steak.

Your barbecue should be built with a raised lip along the front so that you can build up an inch or two of ashes. These quickly become a hot, glowing base almost as soon as you light a fire on top of them, and they save the burning away of much wood.

This is the sort of barbecue we built at Burradoo. Jo Fallon gave much valuable assistance during the hot week end when we brought it as close to completion as ever it will be. But we never did get around to erecting the mechanically operated spit, which was to have straddled the coals and slowly turned whole suckling pigs and baby lambs that were going to be specially fed on milk.

We might as well confess that the back of that barbecue at Burradoo has been waiting for a final layer of stones for the last five years. It has mellowed with the weather and the happy hours which have been spent around it, and it will probably keep on waiting just as it is.

The main thing is that wood burns quickly down to ash in our barbecue, and even when we pile on green tops for that tangy, bushy smell, it never smokes. This might be due to inexpert spaces left between stones during construction.

Sometimes the host stands over the sizzling chops and steak. If the guests please to do so, they may take care of their own grilling.

We cheat with the sausages. No one can barbecue sausages at the same time as other meats without burning the skins to a crisp and losing half the insides. So spread your sausages in a dry baking dish with a few dabs of butter and cook them slowly in the kitchen oven.

As a change from potatoes, or with potatoes, we have a bean dish which adds new relish to a barbecue meal.

CASSEROLED BEANS

1 lb. green lima beans	1 tablespoon vinegar
1 lb. brown kidney beans	2 teaspoons mustard
1 large can Boston baked beans	2 tablespoons brown sugar
¼ lb. bacon	1 tablespoon tomato sauce

Soak the lima and brown beans for 24 hours. One hour before you expect the barbecue to take place, put all three types of beans into a casserole. Lace the beans with the ¼ pound of bacon cut into 3″ lengths. Add vinegar, mustard, brown sugar and tomato sauce.

Put lid on very tight and cook for ½ hour at 350° F. Then reduce the oven to 250° F.

Knowing what barbecues are, you should reduce oven temperature very low after another ½ hour and then you can leave the beans to take care of themselves until you are ready to serve.

Wine in Cooking

In Brussels there's a famous statue of a little boy. It's really a fountain. You know the one that's widely reproduced on postcards with the advice, "Never drink water." That advice needs rounding off with five more words..."Never cook with it, either."

Almost always you can ignore instructions of the average English or American cookbook to use water with meat in cooking. Substitute stock based on the same meat. Or use wine. Red for dark meat, white for light.

If your judgment tells you to use wine, be precise about the quantity. If it becomes necessary to add more, then do remember that if wine is added to the saucepan or casserole during the last hour of cooking, it will give your dish the taste of wine. Only in certain dishes, and mostly sweets, is this desirable. Wine should merge its flavor with that of the meat and so give you that subtle flavor behind a flavor which is French cooking.

A Change from Curry

MOLNAR

A RECIPE FROM RUSSIA, AND ANOTHER FROM HUNGARY,
FOR THE "FORK" MEAL WHICH SEEMS HERE TO STAY

The custom of using forks for eating came to us from
Italy, and was not known in England until the reign of
James I. Silversmiths were quick to see opportunities for
new business. As the kings and queens of England came
and went, additional forks, knives and spoons were invented
to deal individually with everything from oysters to iced
sherbet. By the time the seventh King Edward reigned,
the extent of the table silver to be dealt with at a ten-

course sitting must have sent many a tightly corsetted debutante into a near swoon.

But the servant problem is rapidly taking us back to the single fork that got James from Scotland through every meal.

The fork dinner has evolved from the cocktail party and we are all for it, especially on Sunday nights when we don't want to get out of a relaxed mood and into a black tie.

BEEF STROGANOFF

Buy two and a half pounds of filet of beef or sirloin steak. Trim off all fat, and you should have approximately the two pounds of filet which is the correct proportion of steak for the balance of the ingredients. Pound each piece of filet with a wooden mallet until it is spread out like a pancake and one-quarter inch thick. Then cut into fingers— each about three inches long by three quarters of an inch wide. Melt one-quarter pound of butter in a covered pan. Add a good dessert spoon of chopped onion and stir quickly for two minutes on each side, keeping pieces on the move. Season with salt and pepper.

Remove steak to warm casserole and set aside. Add a half pound mushrooms (minus stalks) to the remaining butter. Return beef to pan, and the very second everything is completely hot again, slowly stir in a half pint of sour cream. Sauté with lid on pan, adding a little more salt and pepper.

The Beef Stroganoff is now ready, but we can't help but think that the dish becomes even richer, and the filet even more meltingly tender, if we transfer it to a moderate oven for three-quarters of an hour before serving.

Beef Stroganoff is served with boiled rice. So put a thick ring of boiled rice around your serving plate and fill the center with this delicious beef before taking it into the table.

Note: Allow a half pound of steak per person.

HUNGARIAN GOULASH

With pimiento, paprika, potato, garlic, onion and butter combining to give it flavor, Hungarian Goulash comes as a complete and highly enjoyable surprise to the taste buds.

Cut two pounds of lean beef into one-and-a-half-inch cubes. Or, alternatively, you can use a pound of beef to one-half pound of pork trimmed of all fat and one-half pound of veal. Season the meat with salt and brown on each side in butter. In another saucepan, sauté four chopped-up onions in a tablespoon of butter until they are limp. Although the onions mustn't "catch," use as little butter as possible as we won't be straining them. To the cooked onions add one small sliced pimiento and then stir in paprika. Add beef, together with three cups of beef stock. (Did you know that at long last a clear beef soup is being sold in cans? This solves the beef stock problem.) Cook very slowly in a tightly covered saucepan for one hour and a half—or until meat is absolutely tender. Serve with noodles which also, and at long last, we can now buy all ready for a ten-minute simmer before serving.

You Can't Cook in More Than Three Ways

HOW TO GET THE MOST OUT OF HOT AIR AND OIL, AND THE NECESSITY FOR SHUNNING WATER

There are just three basic methods of cooking. You subject the materials to be cooked either to hot air, hot oil, or hot water. You can make hot water into steam in a steamer, in a cocotte and in a pressure cooker. But steam acts like water would if water could only get hotter without becoming steam. Each is useful in a different way. It depends entirely on the results you want to get.

Water can never get hotter than 212° F., which is not very hot for cooking. Furthermore, water is a slow conductor of heat. In a laboratory you can take a test tube full of water and boil it at the top while still holding onto the bottom. It transfers its heat very slowly. If you are a fast mover you can put your finger in hot water and plunge it instantly into cold water without a serious burn. You can do it with water, but don't try it with hot oil. If you must experiment, try putting your finger into boiling mercury next, and then boiling lead. You will understand very quickly.

Water does one thing that hot oil and hot air cannot do. It not only cooks the meat, but it dissolves the tissues which bind the muscular fibres together. Thus you can cook a tough chunk of beef or a tough old bird in water or steam. That won't do much to make tender the muscular fibre, but it will dissolve the tissues that hold it together lengthwise. If it is overcooked, the fibres will fall apart like a bundle of faggots when the string is cut.

Water is the cooking method par excellence of amateurs. Most things are rendered tasteless by it. Water cooking has to be studied to be right. All that amateurs seem to succeed in doing is to make things soft. Vegetables should not be cooked in water, except for the woody ones like string beans. The others lose their taste, their nutritive value and their vitamins to the water. That is one reason why the water that has been used for cooking vegetables should be kept for making soup. At least you can get some of the losses back.

Cooking by steam is one of the classic ways of cooking. Before the days of pressure cookers, it was generally done in an iron pot with a concave lid. The small amount of water that covered the tough meat from the cow that was too old to milk, and the vegetables, would form steam which would condense on the lid. From the top it would roll down the sides of the lid and slip gently back into the pot without making a disturbance. For any of those tasty foods that require a long cooking for tenderness, and to let the bouquets mingle, this is ideal. It seems doubtful if pressure cooking will ever replace it.

Pressure cooking is merely a modification of this primitive steam cooking. It is faster, it preserves the vitamins, and it preserves the original taste of the raw materials in the way that steam cooking does and that hot oil and hot air don't. It seems to be too fast for making a dish that requires a long time for the ingredients to mingle and form something new in the way of flavors.

Frying is the art of cooking in boiling fat. Since it can reach a temperature double that of water, it takes some knowing how. Where roasting is generally done in an oven at 325° F., some vegetable oils will go to 450° F. It is essential to know what to cook in hot oil, and, above all, to avoid having any moisture on the food to be cooked. It is also essential that the oil be at its smoking temperature and that it be kept at that temperature during the whole operation. Because of its heat, it is the method used to make crisp foods.

Cooking by hot air is done by fire from above in grilling and by heat all around in roasting. Because air can't transfer its heat as fast as oil, it will take longer to sear the roast. After it is seared, the temperature is generally lowered during the rest of the operation.

One modification of cooking by hot air is in pan frying. Here the food is put in contact with hot metal with an insulating film of fat between them. Flesh has an unhappy tendency to stick to hot metal, otherwise. Certainly it would cook without fat, but it wouldn't come off. You can try that with your finger too, if you didn't burn it in the boiling lead.

MOLNAR

Home at Five Thirty

"How can you produce such a dinner after being at work all day!" You'll find praise like that quite sweet and ever so easy to earn with this four-course dinner for six people that would justify "black tie" on the invitation.

A certain showmanship comes into this dinner. Also some preparation on the night before.

THE MENU

Globe Artichokes with hot melted butter
(Oysters au Naturel if artichokes are out of season).
Steak Diane with Pommes-de-terre Duchesse
French Salad
Cuban Bananas

THE NIGHT BEFORE

All you have to do on the night before is prepare your Duchesse Potatoes. Peel and boil one medium potato for each person. Dry mash them and then add the yolks of two eggs, dropping them in one at a time with plenty of beating in between. Now add enough butter, a teaspoon at a time, to whip the potatoes almost to the point of moistness. Not the speck of a lump may be left in them. Salt and pepper. Then, between the palms of your hands, quickly roll the whipped potatoes into little balls about three quarters of an inch in diameter. Roll each one lightly in flour and put in your refrigerator until the following night. When you arrive home on the following night, remove from the refrigerator and let thaw out for an hour. (If they feel moist, give them another quick last-minute roll in flour.) Start cooking them in very hot deep fat about five minutes before you sit your guests down to dinner. After a minute or so, the potato balls come to the surface and bobble about on top. In a few more minutes they're crisped and golden-brown all over. Lift and drain. The potatoes can wait on grease-proof paper in a mildly warm oven during the first course.

ON THE NIGHT OF THE DINNER

ARTICHOKES. Not for one moment do we mean those knobby little runts of things that look something like potatoes, taste like crushed ants and are sometimes known as Jerusalem artichokes. No! Not those.

The artichokes with which we are commencing our dinner are true globe artichokes. One to each person.

Tie each artichoke around with string in case the coarser outside "leaves" might open up in the saucepan. Drop artichokes into boiling salted water for twenty minutes. Drain. Remove string and serve.

Let's put the coarse outer leaves aside, take those tender inner leaves and dip them into the hot melted

butter which we have spooned onto each plate; then each leaf slides between our closed teeth, leaving behind its delicately flavored pulp.

The leaves rise out of the white heart of the artichoke, and this is the most delicious part of all.

STEAK DIANE. To the best of our knowledge, it was immaculately groomed Tony Clerici, whom we first knew at Romano's, who introduced Steak Diane to this town. You haven't been to Sydney unless you've had Tony himself stand beside your table, deftly prepare this steak in a heavy copper pan, tantalize your appetite with its sizzle and aroma, and then serve you.

Let's do our best to emulate Tony. Our very first rehearsal will reward us, even though we never quite attain Tony's perfection.

One thing to remember! You must use filet. Also get yourself a proper steak mallet in any good kitchenware department. Remove all fat from each filet and hammer out into pancake-size pieces one-quarter inch thin. Rub very lightly with salt and give the ghost of a sprinkle of pepper.

Chop up a large garlic very fine.

Chop up two tablespoons of parsley very fine.

Have a bottle of Worcestershire sauce within hand's reach.

Put at least an eighth of a pound of butter into your pan and be prepared to renew liberally.

When butter is sizzling, drop in your first piece of steak, giving it a quick move so that it won't stick. After forty seconds for underdone, and a minute for medium, turn steak over. Sprinkle liberally with parsley and garlic. Then a moderate dash of Worcestershire sauce—and your butter must be really hot enough to sizzle when the

Worcestershire goes in. Quickly move the steak around to distribute the sauce. Then onto a hot plate with the steak; a generous pouring over it of the sauce from the pan, add the Pommes-de-terre Duchesse, and command the guest of honor to start eating immediately.

There is no time for waiting with Steak Diane. Add more butter to the pan and repeat the procedure one steak at a time.

I worked out this recipe after watching it prepared many times at Romano's, and it mightn't be such a bad idea, at that, if you ordered it there, too, some evening.

You might catch some trick that I missed, but I don't think so.

FRENCH SALAD. Put your salad onto the table as you serve the Steak Diane. As we commenced dinner with artichokes, we have not bothered about a green vegetable for the main course, but as the steak rapidly becomes smaller and smaller on each plate, we can help ourselves to crisp green salad.

Use three parts of the best olive oil to one part vinegar for the salad dressing, not forgetting salt and pepper, and use tarragon vinegar if you can get it.

CUBAN BANANAS. The first thing you do when you reach home on the night of the dinner is prepare this sweet.

Take two bananas for each person, peel and split in halves. Place them, two or three layers according to need, in a casserole dish. On top of each layer generously sprinkle grated orange rind, sugar and powdered cinnamon.

For twelve bananas you would need two tablespoons of butter, broken up into small pieces and distributed through the layers. Add a tablespoon each of orange juice and curacoa.

Put the cover on the casserole and stand aside until just about the time you start to cook your Steak Diane. Then pop the casserole into a 350° F. oven for twenty minutes. If you spend an extra ten minutes talking at the table, it really won't matter. The bananas might go a little floppy, but the flavor seems to improve. In fact, the aroma which meets you when you lift the cover is something the guests should share.

Now another good dash of curacoa, and back into the oven for a few seconds to let the liqueur warm up ready for lighting, but not long enough to evaporate. Put a match to the curacoa-soaked bananas and carry, in flames, to the table.

That's a dinner for six which can be brought to completion in an hour and a half.

Not only does the confidence of experience, of "knowing how" in advance, make such streamlined preparation easy, but you also get real pleasure instead of worry out of all that you're doing even though the guests are arriving and helping themselves to the cocktails.

Twelve Minutes for Spaghetti

...WITH A SAUCE FOR IT, VEAL TUNA FISH TO FOLLOW, AND A SWEET FROM ITALY, TOO!

"Limonaia"—which is "The Lemon Tree Villa"—sits high on a hill outside of Florence.

Nazis occupied it during the war and tore up its elaborately inlaid floors for firewood. Local Communists followed them in and added to the shambles.

Then, after years of absence in Australia, Patricia and Gualti Volterra returned to "Limonaia."

By a miracle, Gualti's two pianos were unscathed, and the villa has been restored to almost all its pre-war beauty.

Somehow we feel that Patricia has one very particular reason to be glad to be back in Florence. At last there's an Italian cook in the kitchen who can be trusted with spaghetti.

Gualti is almost an ascetic at the table. He is the one Italian who never drinks wine.

But spaghetti! That is the weakness of our favorite pianist. It must be just precisely so!

Patricia took us into the kitchen one Sunday night just before she left Australia, and proved that to prepare it properly is almost as simple as making a pot of tea.

Into boiling water that has been generously salted, you toss the spaghetti. Simmer briskly for precisely twelve minutes. You strain it—but in the straining you don't have to go to extremes. Leave a slight moistness, a very slight moistness. This helps the lump of butter you toss in quickly, then toss and toss again, to slither and slide all through the gleaming coils, coating them with gold.

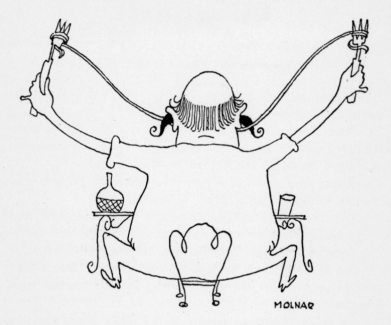

MOLNAR

Serve immediately!

You can serve simply with green butter—chopped parsley dropped into hot melted butter and then poured over the spaghetti.

Or you can add one of the many spaghetti sauces. Finally, and always, a sprinkle of grated Parmesan cheese.

The one thing to remember is that spaghetti must not cook too long or be allowed to stand around before serving. If either of those two things happen, we get that starchy, gluey texture which is found at its worst in our local abomination, the spaghetti sandwich.

Now for those two sauces.

Our sauce is the traditional Ragout which has been

ladled onto spaghetti in Italian homes for generations. To Signora Cattani we express our thanks for this one.

RAGOUT

Take a saucepan—or a small copper pot if you have one—and put in all together a couple of onions cut fine, two or three tomatoes, a couple of cloves of garlic minced fine, and a little parsley—and about half a pound of beef which has been cut up into small squares. Let all this fry with a couple of ounces of butter and a little lard. Let it fry until the meat is cooked and brown and crisp. Then add water or stock—a little at a time—and let it simmer on a low flame. Your sauce forms while it is simmering—the density of the ragout depends on how much liquid you add. If you want it thick, then don't add too much water—or add a teaspoon of flour. Just before using the ragout, stir in a tablespoon of butter—but don't let the butter cook. This will bring up the flavor of the ragout.

Beautiful Eleanor Arrighi, who, like Patricia Volterra, is another Australian girl who has lived in Italy, suggests our main course which now follows.

VEAL WITH TUNA FISH SAUCE

5 lbs. boned loin of veal	1 breakfast cup of olive oil
2 cans tuna fish	1 lemon
6 anchovies	½ cup capers

Boil veal until tender with a little salt in water. Remove when cold, slice thinly and spread on a large dish.

Pass tuna fish and anchovies through sieve until a soft paste, mix in oil and lemon juice, add capers. Pour over sliced cold veal and leave at least 4 hours before eating.

Eleanor also gives us her recipe for a spaghetti sauce. This one introduces bacon, and it is interesting to compare it with the sauce of Signora Cattani, as both ladies are excellent cooks.

SPAGHETTI SAUCE

1 onion	5 large tomatoes
2 cloves garlic	Salt and pepper
¼ cup of olive oil	½ lb. beef round or chuck,
2 slices bacon	ground fine

Mince onion and garlic and put in saucepan with a little oil. When a golden brown, add bacon finely chopped, then the tomatoes which have been peeled and quartered, add the oil and little salt and pepper. Leave cooking for 20 minutes (slowly).

After the veal we have a salad with French dressing and a tasty cheese. Then comes...

ZABAGLIONE

... WHICH IS A SWEET FROM ITALY, TOO!

This froth of egg yolk and wine, light as a twilight breeze, is all that is needed to bring sweetness to the palate as a fine lunch or dinner nears its end.

Zabaglione can be whipped up in a few minutes, and those few minutes are the ones that come immediately before serving. This means leaving the table, and it speeds you along to have someone add the sugar as you whip. So do as Mrs. Frank Tracy did the night she gave me this recipe, and check if there is anybody at the table who would like to see you make it.

ZABAGLIONE

6 egg yolks.
6 sugars measured in broken half egg shells.
6 Marsala (or sweet Sherry) measured as sugar
    in half shells.

Beat egg yolks over boiling water (double boiler), add
sugar and wine alternately, and very gradually. All the
time you keep on beating. The frothing contents of your
saucepan rise up and up until finally they are pure foam.
Add grated lemon peel to taste and serve immediately.

Perfect Balance

IN THE SERVING OF A MEAL
AND WHY THE FRENCH EXCEL AT COOKING

This balance is demonstrated by two lunches and two dinners which have been planned for us by four French wives. Recipes are for eight people.

WHY DO THE FRENCH EXCEL AT COOKING?

We all know good cooks, even excellent cooks, who cannot speak a word of French. Yet why do we leave the homes of our friends who are French with the feeling, and the word feeling is carefully chosen, that we have lunched or dined in much finer style than usual?

The French excel at cooking. Yes, but there is more to it than that. They have given the world its greatest recipes! We'll grant that, too! There comes a third and most important factor—the French wife balances her meal.

The meals of France have light and shade, point and counterpoint of flavor.

Our French wife will plan her meals so that each dish shall be served properly hot or properly chilled. That is one reason why her main meat course is never accompanied by three or four vegetables. Some of those vegetables would have to suffer.

Roast beef most likely comes with its own juice (not thickened), together with chips, crisp and golden on the outside, floury within, and piping hot. Perhaps with this there is a lettuce salad.

Then, with the meat finished, and as a course in their own right, might come the beans. These will be baby beans melting with butter.

If there are four courses, then we can be sure that three of them will be light, although not necessarily as simple as the serving of beans just mentioned.

In these servantless days the meal is also likely to be planned so that much can be done the day before.

The hostess might have to leave the table to attend to the final minutes of a Bearnaise sauce, but even what might seem to be an elaborate meal, when analyzed, will

have only one dish that requires experience, or last-minute attention, and somewhat more than the usual amount of preparation. It is not always the main course that requires the greatest amount of preparation and experience.

This you will now discover in the four quite splendid meals which have been planned for us by our four French wives. They are splendid meals, and if any of our readers commenced the first page of "French Wife" with any thought that this was a book for family cooking, they would have by now changed their minds.

There are two lunches and two dinners. They are planned for special occasions.

The recipes, for which we are truly grateful, are set out precisely and given in full.

One of the four great meats ... beef, veal, lamb and chicken ... has been selected for the main course in each recipe.

As you read through these four meals you will decide, "Ah, that I can do! And that's simple enough." But others, such as the Chicken Quenelles in Mrs. Coleman's luncheon and the Ham Soufflé in the dinner of the Countess D'Espinay, require careful rehearsal. Serve them for the first time with other courses that you could cook blindfolded but for the risk of burning yourself. Rehearsal! Rehearsal! It's the secret of success with any recipe and with any dinner worthy of the name.

First Luncheon

By

MADAME JEAN STRAUSS

Creamed Spinach and Eggs
Coquilles St. Jacques
Veal Foyot
Chicory and Beetroot Salad
Crème Bavaroise

Two sauces of similar nature should never appear on the same menu. "Ah!" you might say after reading the description of this luncheon, "Then why does Madame Strauss use a cream sauce for the spinach of the first course and a cream sauce for the Coquilles St. Jacques which follow?"

"Ah!" we reply. "But the cream sauce required for the first course is so merged with the spinach that by the time it reaches the table it has lost its identity as a sauce!"

CREAMED SPINACH AND EGGS

Prepare 8 heaping tablespoons of spinach from which all water has been pressed.

Make a rich cream sauce. Put 5 tablespoons of butter and 4½ tablespoons of flour into a saucepan and bring together with a wooden spoon over a low flame. Add ¼ cup of milk, then 3/4 cup of cream. Cook gently, stirring occasionally, for 15 minutes over an asbestos mat.

Cut 4 seven-minute eggs into quarters.

Add spinach to sauce and, as soon as spinach has taken up heat, place in a warm dish. Top spinach with eggs and serve.

COQUILLES ST. JACQUES

Make a white sauce using...

6 tablespoons butter	3 cups milk
6 tablespoons flour	½ cup cream

Bring butter and flour together in a saucepan over a low flame. Stir in milk. Then cream. Cook gently for 15 minutes, not forgetting that occasional stir with a wooden spoon.

1 snapper	Lemon juice
2 handfuls peeled shrimp	Fine bread crumbs
½ cup sliced sautéed mushrooms	Butter

Steam a snapper and separate into teaspoon-size flakes. Add shrimp and mushrooms. Add all this to the white sauce plus a squeeze of lemon juice. Place in ramikin dishes. Cover with a sprinkle of bread crumbs and morsels of butter. Place under broiler just barely long enough to delicately brown crust without making it too hard. Then serve. (These can be prepared hours before and set aside to wait upon last-minute heating, but in this case it is necessary to brown them in the oven, as they must be heated right through.)

VEAL FOYOT

The historic Restaurant Foyot closed its doors in the late Thirties. One of the reasons why it will be long remembered is this veal to which Foyot gave his name.

4 or 5 lbs. leg of veal	1 large glass of beef stock or hot water
2 good-sized onions	¼ lb. grated Gruyere cheese
Butter	½ cup bread crumbs
1 large glass of dry white wine	Melted butter
Pepper and salt	

Chop up onions, sauté them in butter until they are soft

and golden but not brown. Add large glass of dry white wine and the same quantity of beef stock or hot water. Pepper and salt. Let boil for 2 minutes, then take off stove. Dip the veal in this liquid until it is thoroughly wet, then place in a baking dish. Rub with pepper and salt. Now mix the Gruyere cheese and bread crumbs together and apply as a good, thick coating all over the joint, pressing firmly into place with the hands just as though you were covering a ham with dough before baking. Now pour enough melted butter all over the coating to moisten it lightly. Take what is left of the liquid and pour this around the joint, but not over it, as the coating must not be disturbed.

Do not baste too often for the same reason. Once or twice is enough, and then only very lightly. Roast for about 3 hours in a 350° F. oven. Then serve.

During the cooking, if your sauce is getting too thick, add a little white wine. But during the last hour, only stock or hot water should be added if required, because if wine is added at this stage its flavor will remain and be too strong.

Serving Veal Foyot. Veal Foyot is served without any vegetable. In this respect it is like duck cooked with orange juice. It needs no other accompaniment.

Carve in good ¼″ slices across the joint. Each slice should be a round of juicy meat surrounded by the Gruyere crust.

CHICORY AND BEETROOT SALAD

We once heard of a French lady who, in her search for chicory, described it to a suburban greengrocer as "like a lettuce with fringe around the leaves." In recent years chicory has grown in popularity. It is now much easier to find. Its leaves are heavier than the lettuce. Its flavor is more robust. Well, then, taking as much chicory as you would take lettuce, and as many cooked beetroots cut into quarters as you would take tomatoes, you toss your chicory and beetroot together with a three-to-one French dressing. Serve.

CREME BAVAROISE AU CAFE

1 cup sugar	1 cup strong black coffee
5 egg yolks	1 pint whipped cream
1 cup milk, heated	Few drops vanilla
1 tablespoon gelatin	¼ lb. sugared almonds
4 tablespoons water	

Mix together in a bowl the sugar and egg yolks, using a wooden spoon. Stir in a cup of milk which has been scalded. Transfer to saucepan and heat over moderate flame, being careful not to let boil.

In the meantime, melt gelatin in hot water and strain into heated contents of saucepan. Transfer back to bowl. Stir in coffee, which should be carefully strained.

Put aside until contents begin to set, giving an occasional stir to prevent a skin from forming. When you decide the setting point has been reached, stir in the pint of whipped cream and vanilla. Place in serving bowl and let stand in refrigerator.

Crush sugared almonds with a rolling pin and sprinkle over the top of the Creme Bavaroise before taking to table.

Second Luncheon

By

MRS. L. R. COLEMAN

Salad Nicoise
Chicken Quenelles
Filet of Beef with Bearnaise Sauce
Potato chips
Fruit Salad

In this luncheon the Chicken Quenelles deserve your very special attention. The quenelles take the flavor of chicken to ambrosian heights. The Bearnaise Sauce to be served with the beef is one of the great sauces of France—if not the greatest.

SALAD NICOISE

1 raw onion	Pepper and salt
3 tomatoes	2 cans tuna fish
2 green peppers	4 hard-cooked eggs
1 celery heart	8 green olives and 8 black olives
4 tablespoons olive oil	1 small can of anchovies
1 tablespoon vinegar	Handful of chopped parsley

Juice of one lemon

Slice the onions into tissue-thin rings. Then cut up tomato in quarters or eighths—never in slices. Discard the hot hearts from the peppers and slice into shreds no thicker than matches. Cut up the heart of the celery. Mix the oil, vinegar, salt and pepper into a dressing and toss through the above ingredients which are already in your salad bowl.

You then cover the mixed salad with tuna fish, hard-cooked eggs cut in four, olives and anchovies. Sprinkle parsley over all of this and add the juice of the lemon—especially over anchovies and fish.

Toss everything at the last moment at the table before serving. Serve with black bread and a white wine of good, strong flavor. Keep your subtler wine for the delicate chicken of the next course, because this noon-time salad is as robust as the natives of Nice, from where it comes.

CHICKEN QUENELLES

1 lb. raw chicken meat (or veal)
5 tablespoons butter
6 egg yolks
½ cup cream

Flour

Pepper and salt
4½ slices white bread
Milk
4 tablespoons butter
6 cups chicken stock

SAUCE

4 tablespoons butter
4 tablespoons flour
1 small can truffles (or mushrooms)

3 cups chicken stock
Butter
Pepper
½ cup cream

Mince the raw chicken as fine as possible. You can even pulverize it lightly after mixing, but be sure to hoard the juice. When it's as close to a paste as you can get it, work in, with a wooden spoon, the butter, egg yolks and the cream. Be quite generous with pepper and salt. Next you take your white bread (no crusts), which you soak in milk and then squeeze very hard. You put the butter in a small saucepan and put your squeezed-out bread in this melted butter. The butter is quickly soaked up and the bread becomes quite dry. Then you work this also into your mixture and put it in the icebox.

Separately you have made a very thick chicken stock with what is left of your chicken carcass. At least 6 cups to begin with.

After thorough chilling, you make a long sausage with your mixture, about the thickness of a cork, rolling out on flour into its sausage shape. Then cut this sausage into 2″ pieces.

Pour your chicken stock into a wide-topped saucepan and put 20 of the little sausages at a time in it. These sausages are your quenelles and they will gradually come up to the top. Reduce the flame and let each batch simmer under cover for 10 minutes. Because they must come to the top and float (that is why you need the wire saucepan), you cannot simmer them all at one time. Put them aside while you simmer the next batch, and in putting them aside you will find that they are quite solid enough to be placed on top of each other.

When all your little quenelles have had their simmering, you will be left with an extra rich chicken stock which we will need for our sauce.

SAUCE FOR CHICKEN QUENELLES

Make a white sauce with the butter, flour, and chicken stock. Separately you have cut up truffles very fine. Lightly sauté them in butter. Sprinkle with pepper and add to sauce, simmering gently for 7 or 8 minutes. Now add the quenelles and simmer for 5 minutes just to heat them through. At the last moment, stir in the cream, allow a moment or two for the cream to take on heat, and serve.

FILET OF BEEF WITH BEARNAISE SAUCE

Pour ¼ lb. melted butter over 2 or 3 lbs. filet of beef. Place in hot oven until it is sizzling well. Then add 2 tablespoons of hot water to sauce, avoiding the meat. Turn oven down to moderate heat and baste every 5 minutes. Cooking time—approximately ½ hour for "underdone."

Remove filet. Put baking dish with its rich juice back over a quick flame. Add salt and pepper and just enough hot water to extend juice to necessary quantity. Do not thicken.

The carving. Cut straight across filet in thick ½" slices. Pour juice from baking dish over each slice. Serve with Bearnaise Sauce.

BEARNAISE SAUCE

¾ cup of dry white wine	Handful chopped parsley
¾ cup of tarragon vinegar	Small lump of butter
1 medium-sized onion, chopped	6 egg yolks
Pepper and salt	Separately — ½ lb. butter

Simmer together the wine, vinegar, onion, pepper and salt, parsley and the butter until the mixture has reduced to half its original quantity. It must simmer very slowly so that the onion can give out all its flavor. Then strain this sauce through tea-strainer—pushing through to extract the last drop of juice but no sediment of parsley or onion. Then add the egg yolks and put sauce on a very, very slow flame, beating constantly with an egg beater. As you beat add, piece by piece, the ½ lb. of butter (soft) which you have cut into little cubes. When sauce is as thick as cream, it is ready to serve.

Note: Tarragon vinegar, which can be obtained locally, has been substituted for the dried tarragon herb, which is difficult to obtain.

Vegetables. One vegetable only. Chip potatoes fried in deep oil.

FRUIT SALAD

Cut fruit in good-size cubes at least one inch square. Two good fruits are often better than a big variety. Oranges capped with strawberries are a delicious combination when in season. Spread sugar over salad before serving. Also juice of a lemon. If you serve champagne with the sweet course, omit lemon and pour a little champagne over fruit just before bringing to table.

First Dinner

By

THE COUNTESS D'ESPINAY

Fish Soup
Ham Soufflé
Chicken à la Crème
French Salad
Riz à l'Imperatrice

FISH SOUP

A Recipe which belonged to Mrs. T. H. Kelly

One night, after a dinner at which this splendid soup had been served, Mrs. Kelly gave the recipe to Louise, remarking that it had been given to her by the Spanish Ambassador. Which Spanish Ambassador? We will never know, but we still call it "The Soup of the Spanish Ambassador."

2½ quarts of water
Equal quantity of bream, snapper, mullet or leather jacket
1 lb. chopped onions
2 cups peeled, chopped and seeded tomatoes

1 cup olive oil
Salt and pepper
½ lb. bread crumbs
4 cloves garlic
2 dozen oysters
1 dozen shrimp
2 cans of salmon, 7-oz. size

2 tablespoons chopped parsley

Put water into a saucepan. Add fresh fish, onions, tomatoes, oil, salt and pepper. Bring to a boil and briskly simmer for 20 minutes. Lift fish and set aside. Strain stock and to it add bread crumbs, garlic, oysters, shrimp and salmon and boil for 5 minutes. Then add fish, which has been freed of all bones. Give fish just sufficient time to take up heat. Drop in parsley. Transfer to tureen.

Note: The bread crumbs absorb olive oil globules left floating on stock and provide the thickening.

HAM SOUFFLE

3 tablespoons butter	1 cup milk
3 tablespoons flour	6 egg yolks
1 lb. ham without fat —	½ cup grated cheese
very finely chopped	8 egg whites

For white sauce melt butter, add flour and stir over low flame until ingredients are well blended. Remove from flame and stir in, little by little, the cup of milk.

Having made white sauce, stir in chopped ham followed by the egg yolks and grated cheese. Heat the oven to a temperature of 425° F. At the last moment, fold lightly into your mixture the egg whites, beaten stiff but not dry. Pour mixture into a greased oven dish, leaving about half of the space to rise. Keep in oven for 35 minutes without opening door (once you've gained confidence). Then serve at table immediately. Note that when adding ham, or any other extra to a soufflé, the soufflé will not rise to the dizziest heights. Nevertheless, this ham souffle will be light and fluffy, providing you are careful to have your oven temperature carefully set.

CHICKEN A LA CREME

2 roasting chickens	2½ glasses of dry white wine
3 medium-sized onions	½ pint cream

Cut up your raw chickens into 6 pieces. (Put the carcasses aside.) Brown each piece of chicken in butter. Remove from pan and put aside in a warm casserole dish. Sauté the onion, chopped very fine, in the same butter, adding extra if necessary. Onions must not be allowed to catch the smallest burn. When soft and golden brown, add the white wine to pan and let it bubble up. Pour this liquid over chicken in casserole dish, removing with a wooden spoon any rich "leavings" sticking to bottom of pan.

Add pepper and salt. Add one small piece of thyme and bay leaf. Place the left-over chicken carcasses on the top so they can add their juice. Cover casserole dish and let cook slowly for about 45 minutes.

When ready to serve, take all the pieces of chicken out, put them on a dish and keep them hot. Throw carcasses away.

To the sauce left in casserole add cream and let it simmer until sauce is thick. (If sauce needs reducing, do so before stirring in cream.) Also add a little chopped parsley. Pour sauce over your hot chicken and send to table.

Serve with noodles and young green peas.

FRENCH SALAD

A simple salad of lettuce tossed with a French dressing of three parts olive oil to one part tarragon vinegar. Sometimes the Countess varies her salad by using chicory as well as lettuce, together with some avocado and halved hard-cooked eggs.

RIZ A L'IMPERATRICE

Circumstantial evidence suggests that this rice was dedicated to the lovely Empress Eugenie. It towers above all other rice sweets as an Empress above her subjects and, bringing our feet back to the kitchen floor, it is to be prepared hours in advance of the dinner.

Cooked rice
1 cup custard
½ cup diced glazed fruit

2 teaspoons Kirsch
(or Maraschino)
1½ cups heavy cream

Glazed cherries, almond halves

First of all, let's cook the rice the way the Countess does it, and soak the glazed fruit in Kirsch for at least 2 hours.

The Countess cooks rice in the following manner as the basis for quite a number of sweets. It must be prepared over a very low flame or else in a double boiler.

1 cup rice	½ teaspoon salt
4 cups milk, scalded	Piece of vanilla bean
8 tablespoons sugar	(or a little vanilla extract)
2 tablespoons butter	6 egg yolks, slightly beaten

Wash rice in cold water, put in a saucepan and cover well with water. Bring to a boil, turn off heat and let stand 5 minutes. Drain in a sieve and rinse by letting cold water run through the rice. Return to pan and add milk, sugar, salt and vanilla bean. Bring to a boil, add butter, cover pan and simmer very gently about ½ hour. (Or cook in top of double boiler about 45 minutes or until rice is done.) Shake grains to separate and then combine with egg yolks. Allow to cool thoroughly.

There is your rice, ready to combine with the custard.

CUSTARD

This is a custard mixture combined with gelatin which is used for the foundation of many sweets. As the mixture sets or starts to become thickened, it must be watched rather closely. If it becomes too stiff before folding in the cream or other ingredients, the result will be streaky with gelatin and uneven in texture.

⅔ cup sugar	2 tablespoons water
1½ egg yolks	2 cups milk
1 tablespoon unflavored gelatin	2 pieces vanilla bean (or a little extract)

Add gelatin to water and let stand to soften. Work up sugar and egg yolks with a wooden spoon until smooth and creamy. Scald milk and vanilla bean together and then add to yolk mixture little by little. Return to saucepan and cook slowly, stirring constantly until it comes to the boiling point. Do not allow to boil. Remove vanilla bean (or add extract). Add gelatin in water. Cool, stirring vigorously at first and then from time to time to prevent crust from forming on top.

While rice is still warm, combine with the custard. Add the diced glazed fruit with Kirsch to rice mixture. Whip cream until stiff and fold into mixture. Place in serving bowl.

Decorate surface of rice with glazed cherries and almond halves. Chill thoroughly before serving.

Second Dinner

MADAME PAUL PELLIER

Potage Santé
Vol-au-vent Financière
Saddle of Lamb with Pommes-de-terre Duchesse
Asparagus Tips
Salad
Crepes Suzette

Every week-end Madame Pellier prepares a demi-glace. This is an extremely rich stock which can be kept in the refrigerator. Then as the need arises during the following week, Madame Pellier takes a soup spoon or two of the demi-glace and adds it to casserole, vol-au-vent or any other dish which will be improved by its concentration of flavor.

So before we present this dinner, we give you Madame Pellier's own recipe for...

....Demi-glace. Fill a baking dish with bones of veal and beef. Add two sliced carrots and two sliced onions. Cook in oven for one hour—very slowly, as we do not add liquid at this stage. Then add a tomato and a small bunch of celery. Cook for one more hour very slowly. Then put in big casserole. Cover with water. Season with salt and pepper. Simmer for four hours. Remove bones. Make a thickening with two tablespoons of butter and a tablespoon of flour. Stir this into juice. Then strain through sieve. Cool and keep in refrigerator.

POTAGE SANTE

Literally translated—health soup. Wash thoroughly a medium-sized bunch of watercress. Cut fine. Place in saucepan with five potatoes cut fine. Add one quart water. Simmer for two hours. Strain through sieve. Reheat for ten minutes.

In your warmed soup tureen, drop the yolks of two eggs and two tablespoons of cream. Pour soup over this. Serve with croutons which have been fried in butter.

VOL-AU-VENT FINANCIERE

Fry two sweetbreads of lamb or veal in a casserole or saucepan. As soon as cooked, put aside to keep warm. Bring four tablespoons of demi-glace to a boil for a minute, strain and set aside. In a second casserole, place the contents of a small can of truffles, the heads of one dozen French canned mushrooms, one-half pound of chicken livers and three tablespoons of Madeira. Boil this with lid on for a few seconds and then add to it the sauce left from the cooking of the sweetbreads.

Simmer for a few minutes, then return everything to casserole containing the sweetbreads in which a tablespoon of butter has been heated. Stir for a moment, making sure all is heated, transfer to puff pastry cases and serve. Order your puff pastry cases from a pastry cook. Those which are about five inches in diameter are the most suitable size for individual servings, or one large case may be used.

Madame Pellier also includes six cockscombs in the filling when obtainable from her William Street poulterer. These she bleaches by boiling for an hour in water, lemon juice and flour. They are then gently simmered for four hours in stock and after this they are ready for inclusion in the Vol-au-vent.

SADDLE OF LAMB

Take a double loin of spring lamb and rub with salt and pepper. Tie it with string. Butter the top and bake in moderate oven, 325° F., basting with butter at frequent intervals.

Madame Pellier usually serves saddle of lamb with asparagus tips and Pommes-de-terre Duchesse (see page 44).

CREPES SUZETTE

The batter:

½ cup twice-sifted flour	1½ cups milk
¾ teaspoon salt	4 tablespoons melted butter
4 eggs (if smallish use five)	2 teaspoons grated lemon rind
1 liqueur glass Grand Marnier	

Mix flour and salt. Combine eggs and milk. Add flour and beat until smooth. Add melted butter, grated lemon rind and a liqueur glass of Grand Marnier. Let stand for at least 1 hour. Then strain if the least sign of a flour particle remains.

The cooking of the crêpes. Very lightly smear a small frying pan with butter. Heat pan, add a pea of butter if necessary, but remember there must be absolutely no butter fluid. Then drop a tablespoonful of batter into pan, holding pan slightly above flame and flicking from side to side in a circular fashion so that batter quickly spreads all over pan. It becomes golden-brown quickly. Then turn and cook on the other side.

The sauce and the flames. When all the crêpes are cooked, place them on a long metal plate, warm it over flame lamp. Sprinkle sugar on top, add a liqueur glass of Cognac, two liqueur glasses of Grand Marnier and the juice of one mandarin or orange. Put a light to the liqueur and serve the crêpes as they are flaming.